THE FIT FOODIE
MEAL
PREP
PLAN

DEDICATION

This book is for you.

You, who have picked this up and given me a chance to change the way you work in the kitchen. You, with real-life commitments, a social life, a family, and probably zero time to really be reading this (did you feed the dog?). I'm so happy you're here, prioritizing something just for you.

Like you, I'm juggling a million things. Businesses, a degree, my mental health, working out, traveling, yada yada yada. There've been moments when I've mastered it all, and moments when I've royally—and publicly—failed.

I am so incredibly grateful to every subscriber, follower, reader, and friend who has supported me on this journey. You've read my many ramblings (including this one), and I dig that I can offer something back to you in the following pages. Even if it really is just an enthusiastic smile and a delicious quiche.

Thank you for helping me create a career beyond my wildest dreams.

Sally

@thefitfoodieblog

THE FIT FOODIE
MEAL
PREP
PLAN

EASY STEPS TO FILL YOUR FRIDGE FOR THE WEEK

SALLY O'NEIL

the *fit* foodie

Contents

Let's Make This Simple

Even with a lovely home office, I'm writing this at a slightly sticky table in my local library, with a group of noisy children in the background. Why? Because I get distracted by stuff—life stuff that I'm sure you deal with too: laundry, phone calls, reorganizing the spice rack thirty times a year, the siren song of Netflix. We're ALL trying to figure out how to do life—a happy, healthy life—and do it with some balance.

Let's be honest: being healthy can be pretty time-consuming. All that yoga, hours at farmers' markets, squeezing your own green juices, and then meal planning is all a bit much. When time is in short supply, all of this can get pushed into the back seat. Even as a food blogger, I can't honestly say that I cook myself a meal from scratch every night. I've got shit to do, and that doesn't involve spending hours at my stove.

While I'm single-handedly trying to build three businesses (which generally consists of Googling everything), completing a nutrition degree, and trying to explore more of the world, I also want to look after my body. I want to feel good while I tackle my to-do list, and I know you do too, but sometimes that goal can feel pretty elusive.

So while I haven't got all the answers, I'm here to share my favorite food hacks: the tricks and tips I've learned that make healthy food SIMPLE.

My method is this: prep it, batch it, store it, assemble it. Okay, the prep might take a bit of time (we're talking two hours a week, tops), but, short of ordering takeout every night, you're not going to find a faster way to eat home-cooked, healthy food. This is the shortcut. This un-cooking cookbook aims to help you claw back time for actually important life stuff.

Now, we're wasting valuable time. In the words of the great Macklemore: Let's eat.

Sally x

Why Meal Prep?

We all seem to have less and less time, and when we're pressed for time, the first things to go are sleep and cooking. While I can't help you with getting more Zs, I can save you time AND money by teaching you the foundations of meal prep.

We seem to get by on less sleep and more coffee, less cooking and more takeout. The end point is the same, but quality of life takes a hit. What you put into your mouth has a huge effect on your weight and physical health. Exercise is an awesome way to improve things, but it can't undo a bad diet. Eating well improves your mental health as well; when you eat good food, you feel better about your choices and happier with the way your body feels.

Healthy meals need to be easy to prepare and readily accessible if you want to have a chance of sustaining a balanced, nutritious diet. Once you have a few simple cooking methods and systems under your belt, endless meal combinations will be open to you.

I'm a passionate advocate of prepping food for the week ahead. When I talk about prepping, I don't mean spending your entire weekend making "all the things." What I'm talking about is the intentional action of making a couple of hero foods that can be used in multiple dishes throughout the week. Every now and then I make other things in bulk so I can freeze them, ready to pull out whenever I need. If you can get into the bulk-cooking mind-set, you'll begin to spend less time in the kitchen, yet have more food ready to eat in your fridge or freezer when you need it.

When I started planning meals with whole foods, I felt overwhelmed. It wasn't until I learned to cook some hero proteins (Step 1), created recipes that I could batch-make and stash (Step 2), and then learned the art of "food assembly" (Step 3) that I managed to get plenty of variety into my diet with minimal cooking time. I'm definitely not going to win any awards for reinventing the cooking wheel, but I sure as hell can teach you how to turbo-charge your meal prep to work faster and smarter.

If you want fine-dining options to wow your highbrow guests, you've picked up the wrong book. Go see a celebrity chef and set aside a day with your dry-ice packs. Meal planning isn't about creating super-fancy or impressive meals every night; it's about cutting down your daily cooking time and taking back those precious minutes for the important stuff, while still eating well.

Five benefits of meal prep

1 Saves time
2 Saves money
3 Reduces waste
4 Keeps your health on track
5 Helps with portion control

How to Put It All Together

To save your sanity, you're not going to be batch-making almond milk and raw nut butters, soaking your own legumes, or making other things you can access easily and cost-effectively from a store. There's also no place here for anything dehydrated, house-fermented, or with a million superfood ingredients. It's a headache, it's time-consuming, and it's super-frustrating if it's just not your jam. Burning precious time in the kitchen is not the aim of the game here. This is fast-action food assembly.

What's meal prep about?

The goal of meal prep is to cook food in advance so that you can assemble meals with little to no effort during your busiest times of the week. Rather than cooking oats every morning, you prepare five servings in one go to last you the entire workweek. It saves you a heap of time when you're at your busiest, and also stops you from reaching for unhealthier options.

Some people love to portion out their meals so they're ready to grab and go, whereas others are happy with a little assembly when hunger strikes. Either way, you'll be making your time in the kitchen far more efficient and saving time for stuff that really matters.

There's nothing stopping you from popping to the store for a decent ready-made pesto or a jar of pickles. SHORTCUTS ARE OKAY. In fact, I've listed some of my fave Supermarket Saviors on pages 28–29. Everything here is optional and designed to make healthy eating as simple and tasty as possible throughout your workweek.

A lot of recipes in this book offer two or three options. That's because once you've mastered the basics, I want you to be inspired to try assembling them in different ways. It's time-saving and avoids the dreaded food fatigue from eating the same thing three days in a row. YAWN.

IT REALLY IS AS SIMPLE AS . . . .

Step **1** → *Step* **2** → *Step* **3**

You're going to start by prepping the main event—the yummiest parts of the dish—in Step 1. This is where you really learn the skills for prepping a few good basics that can be used over and over.

Step 2 will have you batch-baking and making snacks and meals that can be eaten right away, or refrigerated and frozen for later use.

Step 3 is where you'll get inspiration for putting all of this together into a zillion combos so you'll never have to eat the same dish night after night. It's called food assembly, because that's all you're required to do.

*Shortcuts are okay!
See pages 28-29 for some
of my faves.*

Getting Started

You know those people who can rustle up an amazing meal when their fridge is seemingly empty? That's the future you. Hey there, resourceful culinary genius!

Making a meal plan might sound like a time drain when you're super-busy. I get it; but trust me when I say it's one of the most impactful ways to organize your life. Here are some quick and simple ways to improve your meal-planning prowess.

1

TAKE STOCK

Run to your pantry, fridge, and freezer and take note of what you already have.

2

SELECT + TEXT

Flip through this book and add a few sticky notes (or just fold the corners down . . . I'll never know) on the recipes you already have ingredients for. If you're missing a few key things, text a quick list to yourself so you can remember what you need next time you go shopping. If you have some key ingredients but are just missing the inspiration for putting it together, then head to Step 3 of this book.

3

WRITE IT DOWN

Grab a notebook (see Tip) and write out the days of the week, then write down your meal ideas using the food you have on hand. Make sure to include a "leftovers buffet" night to eat up anything that's left. You can always throw in a can of tuna or a hard-boiled egg to make it a more complete meal. Congrats—you just did your meal planning!

Tip

Use a notebook to make your meal plans; avoid using scrap paper, or you'll end up losing your hard work. Your notebook will be your gold mine for ready-made meal plans. As you go along, you'll refine them to include your fave options and those that work best for your time allowance. Ideally, you'll learn fifteen to thirty delish, hardworking recipes that you'll use as staples, mixing it up with a few newbies every so often to avoid food fatigue.

In the vein of working smarter, not harder, you can reuse these meal plans on rotation. More time saved!

4

MAKE TIME

Allocate some time in your schedule to prep and store your key ingredients. If you only have five minutes to chop veggies, do that.

Scribble in your notebook what prep is required, starting with the most time-consuming tasks first. I find that this helps keep me focused during prep time and gives me an efficient work flow: what to make first, second, and last.

5

COOK ONCE, EAT TWICE

Whenever you prep something by mixing, blending, or adding heat, you're going to make more than one portion . . . always.

Most of the meals (or the components of them) in this book are freezable or will last up to a week in the fridge. This ensures that you won't get bored. Food fatigue is a real thing, and it will derail your efforts. That's why assembly of different food combos and dressings is so important. But more on that in Step 3.

6

ENJOY YOUR SPARE TIME

As well as knowing that you've got a lot of healthy meal options ready to go, you just bought yourself a whole lot of extra leisure time!

It always helps to have a clean kitchen with your meal-prep containers washed and ready to go.

Tips for Success

These are a few things I've learned about planning ahead that will definitely make your meal prep easier.

Start small

Please don't flip over to the next few pages and feel overwhelmed by the need to make eight different recipes for the week ahead. Start small, and multitask. If you have a spare ten minutes (come on, I know you do), you have time to prep your breakfasts for the entire week with a big batch of overnight oats. Work with the time you have and the ingredients you have.

Try by picking a few simple recipes without many ingredients, and whatever you don't have in the house, stick on a shopping list. You'll find it easier if you pick a few recipes that utilize the same ingredients, and it saves on food waste too. You'll get the hang of this quickly.

Keep it simple

If I were here to tell you how to make extravagant meals, you'd be hatin' on me for the time and cost involved. Simplicity is our key focus. That doesn't mean bland, repetitive food, but it does mean getting into the habit of preparing ingredients simply and then amping up flavor with sauces, herbs, and a bit of imagination. To make sure you have plenty of variation, we'll focus on perfecting the main protein event of meals—think chicken, fish, tofu—and then learn how to assemble these super-quickly in a number of different ways so you don't get sick of the same stuff.

Get creative

Experiment with swapping ingredients listed in the recipe for what you have available: whatever's in season, your favorite veggies, or what's in your pantry. I'm not asking you to go out and buy a whole new pantry of ingredients—I'm trying to help you save money and time, not spend more of both. If a recipe calls for dried oregano and you only have paprika, just switch it!

Multitask

Pick recipes with different cooking methods so you can multitask. That way, something can be baking in the oven while you're poaching something else on the stovetop. Start on the stuff that takes the longest to cook and finish with the simplest prep. You'll save a lot of time this way and get more food prepped!

Roast different foods with the same cooking time together. Pairing root veggies (those that are grown underground), such as carrots, sweet potatoes, and parsnips, in the same roasting pan can save time and add variety. Fast-cooking veggies (usually softer and grown aboveground) can be paired too: think asparagus, cherry tomatoes, and zucchini.

Don't be afraid to take shortcuts

Contrary to popular belief, you're not actually Superwoman. There are some things you just won't have time for, and when that time comes, there's no need to beat yourself up for taking a shortcut. I've listed some of my time-saving tips on pages 24–25.

Master class

Instead of cooking entire meals, the focus of this book is to break them down into common parts that you can cook separately and ahead of time. This means you can mix and match buffet-style and really focus on combining different foods at each meal. We'll get into this in Step 3, where you'll be looking to pick foods from different categories (carbs, fats, and proteins) to make a balanced, complete meal.

If you're new to this, start by prepping just a few days' worth of meals.

Nutrition 101

Before you dive into DIY Kingdom and start to prep your meals like a boss, you need to know how to build a balanced meal. "Balance" refers to the type and amount of macronutrients on your plate. There are three macros you need to include in each meal, and they all serve different purposes.

It's highly likely that you're going to flip through this cookbook, like many others that have graced your hands before it, for meal inspiration. You want pretty food pictures, some easy tips on saving time, and a couple of winning, healthy dinner ideas that you can rustle up on the fly. You'll then go into the kitchen and decide what is most convenient to make with one of my ideas as a loose plan for the dish.

That's perfect. This isn't a dogmatic recipe guide or diet. You're nailing meal prep if you want to go it alone and DIY—it means you're integrating it into your life as a good habit on the regular and are willing to get creative. Not eating the same thing every day is the only way a meal prep system will work for you. Variety is the key to success (and the spice of life, obvs). It's better for your body, too, when you're packing in a wider range of vitamins and minerals from different foods rather than sticking to the same stuff. #EatARainbow and all that.

So what are the three macronutrients, and how do you include them in your diet? They are carbohydrates (carbs), proteins, and fats.

Why do we need all three in a meal for balance? In essence, it's related to how quickly your body burns through them. The quickest to break down (or burn) are carbs and then proteins, with fats being the slowest. If you really want to get into that, read on. I love to be armed with all the info so I can make the best of every meal, and it makes it easier to choose a healthy, satisfying meal when you eat out (or order in).

Carbs

Your body burns carbohydrates first; they're broken down into glucose in the body to provide its primary source of fuel. Not all carbs are created equal. There are subcategories (are you zoning out yet?) of "Simple Carbs" and "Complex Carbs." Simple carbs burn faster than complex, because they've got only one or two chemical bonds holding their structure together. Oooh, this is like a science lesson . . . you're SO welcome.

White sugar is one such simple carb. It actually starts out as brown sugar. MIND BLOWN? When the molasses is removed, the simple sugar crystals are left. White rice is another simple carb, with the bran and germ removed from its original brown-rice state. Natural simple carbs exist, too: certain veggies (white potato, I'm looking at you), some fruits, and milk.

When you eat a simple carb, it's broken down super-fast, and the glucose is funneled into the bloodstream quickly. A rush of glucose hits your bloodstream = hello blood-sugar spike! On the other hand, complex carbs (often referred to as "good" carbs) are the ones that take longer for your body to digest and break down. Think sweet potato, whole grains (like brown rice), steel-cut oats, and pumpkin. Chemically, they have three bonds to break down, which just takes longer. That means blood-sugar levels remain more stable, because the glucose is slower to reach the bloodstream.

Okay, enough of that. Let's just say complex carbs are your friends; simple carbs less so. Limit them where you can, but also don't be insane. Cow's milk isn't going to kill you. (Unless it's curdled. Tip: Don't store milk in a hot car.)

Proteins

Next up in the fuel-burning tank is protein. Proteins have a more complicated structure than carbs, being composed of many little building blocks called amino acids. Protein bonds need acid to break them because they're difficult to denature. That's why we have some lovely hydrochloric acid in our stomachs to mix around with our food to break it down. Protein is loved by gym-goers and dieters alike, primarily because it helps with muscle repair. A higher muscle ratio in the body means a higher basal metabolic rate (your metabolism rate at rest) and therefore more calories burned doing absolutely nothing more than the average person does. It's really a lot more complicated than that, but for now, we just need to know that adequate protein is important to keep us healthy.

Fats

Fat takes the longest to digest and helps to delay stomach emptying: we stay full for longer! It also has the highest kilojoule count per gram, so we don't need tons of it to sustain us. It helps our bodies make use of any fat-soluble vitamins we eat. Without the fat, as the name suggests, these vitamins (namely A, D, E, and K) become difficult for our bodies to use—so think of fat as a tasty vitamin carrier, if you will. Without going into the science of fats, because, well, your life is passing you by, let's just say there are some fats that are better for us than others. Generally speaking, unsaturated fats are better for us than the saturated kind. (There's a bit of a debate about coconut oil, but you can do some research on this for yourself, using reputable sources. I like to use it in baking, where it adds flavor and texture.)

CARBS

Primary digestion location: begins in the mouth (with saliva) and continues in the stomach.

———

Totally demonized in recent years by the keto movement, and prior to that by the Atkins Diet, carbs really do get a bad rap. They are, however, your body's primary source of fuel, and your brain needs them to function, peeps. In fact, your alertness and concentration depend on them. You'll get them from starchy veggies, brown rice, sourdough bread, oats, and the like. Don't be a carbophobe.

PROTEINS

Primary digestion location: stomach.

———

Protein is the main component of muscles, bones, skin, and hair. Protein burns more calories when it's digested because the chemical bonds are a bitch to break down. It increases the production of two hormones that help you feel full and satisfied, and it also reduces the hunger hormone. Double win. Find it in meat, oats, seafood, tofu, nuts, protein powder (surprise!), beans, and other legumes.

FATS

Primary digestion location: small intestine.

———

Fats help our bodies to regulate hormones, help to insulate the body to keep us toasty warm, give us shiny hair and glowing skin . . . among a million other cool things. Contrary to the low-fat diet dogma, eating fat does not make you fat—*eye roll*. If that were true, I would be an avocado. Fats are necessary for us to absorb certain vitamins and work wonders for our satiety. Some fats are more awesome than others. Oily fish, avocados, olive oil, nuts, and seeds are fab natural sources.

Build Your Meals Like a Boss

Now that you know WHY we need balanced meals, here's how to build them.

1
CHOOSE A FRESH BASE
Such as salad greens or veggies

→

2
CHOOSE A PROTEIN
Think tuna, chicken, eggs, or tofu

→

3
ADD COMPLEX CARBOHYDRATE
Pumpkin, sweet potato, and whole grains all count

4
ADD SOME HEALTHY FAT
Avocado, nuts, seeds

→

5
DRIZZLE WITH DELICIOUS DRESSING
(see pages 122–23) or just use plain olive oil

→

6
ADD SOME FLAVOR BOMBS
I love herbs and chili (or see pages 20–23 for other ideas)

= *Boss meal*

5
Drizzle with DRESSING

2
PROTEIN

1
Fresh BASE

3
Complex CARBS

4
Healthy FAT

6
Add FLAVOR BOMBS

Flavor Bombs

I buy copious amounts of these staples to add epic flavor intensity to any dish. I call them "flavor bombs"; just a small amount goes a long way and can take a meal from drab to fab in seconds.

	DESCRIPTION	NOTES
Salt	Salt isn't actually a flavor but a flavor enhancer. Just a pinch reduces bitterness and increases sweet, sour, and umami. Salt gets a bad rap because it can contribute to high blood pressure, but our bodies do need some for electrolyte balance.	Pink salt is particularly good because it contains many beneficial minerals. I've been known to eat pink salt flakes directly from the saltcellar, so maybe don't follow my lead on that one. *Confession*
Black pepper	I'm actually not a big pepper fan (cringe), but it does have a place in my kitchen. Just a pinch can increase the intensity of flavors.	The potassium in pepper can stimulate digestion and discourage bloating.
Chili, fresh or dried	A little goes a long way here. Even if you're not big on spicy food, just a pinch can boost the flavor of a meal tenfold.	Chili can suppress appetite and relieve muscle aches and cramps.
Miso	This salty fermented soybean paste adds delicious umami flavor to any dish. Don't be afraid to add it to sweet things, too, for balance. Check out the Banana PB and Miso Smoothie on page 184.	Miso contains beneficial bacteria, just like yogurt and kombucha!
Garlic	This traditional aromatic is used as a base for many flavorsome dishes. Think dips, pasta sauces, stir-fries. It's thought to help lower blood pressure.	Fresh is best, but I'll turn a blind eye if you want to use the crushed stuff from a jar, or even dried flakes. I think that grating garlic is a total pain in the ass.

	DESCRIPTION	NOTES
Spring onions	Sometimes called scallions in the USA and shallots in Australia, these are the long green onions with white tips.	Thinly slice and refrigerate in a glass container, ready to scatter over salads, meat, and fish.
Cinnamon	Famous for its sweet profile, cinnamon is totally underrated in savory dishes. Add it to foods that are high in natural sugar (such as bananas or dates) to help reduce the immediate impact on your blood-sugar levels.	Cinnamon has the highest antioxidant value of any spice.
Cilantro	These fragrant, citrusy leaves are awesome toppers to almost any savory dish. Mix into salads, mash into avocado, or scatter over dinner. Cilantro is an antioxidant powerhouse that helps improve digestion.	I once heard on a morning TV show that we are born with taste buds that either love or hate cilantro, depending on genetics. I used to pick it out of every meal, and now I LOVE it, so I think I've debunked that theory.
Citrus	Lemons, limes, oranges, and grapefruits are delicious in salad dressing and add acidity and tangy flavor.	These guys are a great source of vitamin C to strengthen the immune system and help keep skin smooth.
Paprika	A spice made from ground capsicums (bell peppers).	Sweet and smoked paprika varieties are available, and both add delicious earthy flavors to food.
Sriracha	A type of hot sauce that originated in Thailand. I love it because it usually has very minimal added sugar (be sure to check the label, though).	Great for adding heat to dressings, meat, and everything in between.
Capers	These delicious little green balls are actually unripened flower buds, pickled in brine or dried.	They add a lemony, salty flavor boost to any savory dish, particularly fish, pasta, and sauces.

Clever stuff

Simple Shortcuts

We're trying to make everything here as efficient as humanly possible. In a perfect world, we'd all have plenty of time to make our own nut milks, salad dressings, and fish stock from scratch. Reality check: unless I dedicate a whole day to meal prep, this isn't going to happen. If you need to make shortcuts to save even more time, these are some smart choices.

Grains Microwavable rice or quinoa packets are fine if you're in a hurry.

Nut milk Buy UHT nut milk. Making your own is kind of a bind if you don't have a total love for it. Avoid brands with added carrageenan, oils, and sugar.

Spice mixes These are easy to pick up in most stores. Check the ingredients to ensure there's no added sugar: it's lurking everywhere.

Sauces and dressings You can absolutely keep it simple, if making a dressing from scratch is in your too-hard basket. You definitely have the energy to pinch your fingers together and squeeze a wedge of lemon or lime—a great alternative to an elaborate dressing, as is a drizzle of olive or avocado oil.

Trail mix Can't be bothered to make your own? WHY ARE YOU EVEN HERE? Kidding. Just make sure there are no added oils or lots of sugar—they're often hiding.

Spiralized veggies

If you haven't jumped on the bandwagon and smugly bought a cheapo spiralizer on the Internet, you're allowed to buy ready-made spiralized veggies from the store. Or, if you DID jump on the bandwagon and then realized that said cheapo spiralizer was total garbage because it was so badly made, you're also allowed to buy ready-made spiralized veggies. We've all been there.

I would add that pre-chopped veggies such as pumpkin and broccoli are a good option, but if you really don't have time to push a knife through some vegetables, you probably don't have time to be reading this book, either.

Stock

In all honesty, making my own stock or even just remembering to reserve the cooking liquid is sometimes beyond my capacity. I keep a carton of liquid stock in my cupboard for emergencies. Stock cubes do the trick, too. No judgment. Keep your eye on the sodium content, though—many are super salty.

Frozen cooked shrimp

I have a stash of these in my freezer and I ain't ashamed to say it. I can defrost a handful in ten minutes by sticking them in a colander and running room-temp water over them. When I'm feeling super lazy, they're a tasty lean protein option that requires zero cooking. See page 174 for ways to use them in combo plates.

Vegetable rice

Replacing carb-laden rice with finely chopped veggies such as broccoli and cauliflower adds an extra serving of vegetables and reduces carbs in one go. Don't have a blender? Just hate washing the veggies? That's totally fair. Save yourself ten minutes and just buy the ready-made stuff.

Microwave myth buster

Think microwaves nuke your food? Microwave technology channels radio waves to excite the molecules in the food, causing them to vibrate and build thermal energy (heat). It's true that some nutrients, such as vitamin C, are affected by heat; however, cooking food faster in a microwave can mean less heat exposure than other cooking methods such as boiling. It makes sense, then, that vitamin C and other water-soluble nutrients are actually better preserved when using a microwave to cook food. Who knew?

My Favorite Snacks

Snacks shouldn't be complicated. The simpler the choice (effortless if possible), the more likely you'll make a good one. So stock up your fridge with these grab-and-go goodies.

Boiled eggs
(see page 44)

Also touted as "nature's multivitamin," eggs make healthy, portable snacks. Boil up a dozen for the week; chop them and throw them on top of salads, or just grab and go when hunger hits. Don't forget a sprinkle of salt.

Blueberries + raspberries

Berries are the perfect snack when you're craving something sweet. While strawbs totally have a place in my heart (and fridge), I want to be able to throw stuff in my mouth without chopping it up or dripping juice down my shirt (which happens most of the time).

Hummus + veggies
(see page 86)

Once your fridge is like a salad bar (we're getting to that; hold tight), you can just grab a handful of fresh veggies and dunk them in hummus for a speedy, nutritious way to fill up. Hummus is packed with fiber that slows the digestion, keeping your tummy from rumbling for a while longer.

Progurt

Protein yogurt: one of the mainstays of my snack cycle because it kicks any sweet cravings and fills me up for hours. If you can't tolerate dairy, look for lactose-free options or go for coconut yogurt. Prep a family-size tub in advance or just mix as you need: 1 scoop of protein powder (about 1 oz or 25 g) mixed with 6½ oz (180 g) of yogurt usually does the trick, but you can add more or less if you like. Look for protein powders that are naturally sweetened and minimally processed.

Bliss balls
(see page 146)

Indulge your sweet cravings the healthy way with portable protein balls. Skip the ready-made ones that so often have added preservatives and flavors. I love to batch-make and freeze mine.

Nuts

Just 1 oz (30 g) of your favorite nuts (or nut butter) makes for an awesome, nutrient-rich snack.

Supermarket Saviors

For those days when you get to work and realize you've forgotten your lunch, or you just can't seem to get organized. You don't need to run to the nearest fast-food outlet; your supermarket has some super-handy and healthy goodies to buy on the fly. Get in there and get some.

Protein bars or balls

Look for low-sugar, natural options with only a handful of ingredients. Most are date-based, so can be on the sugary side. Eat in moderation: some are candy bars in disguise.

Nuts

Ideally opt for the raw versions: the ingredients list shouldn't contain anything but the nuts and maybe a pinch of salt.

Hard-boiled eggs

Most supermarkets sell hard-boiled eggs now, so jump on them for a dose of healthy fats and protein. Win! There is a method for boiling a fresh egg in a teakettle, but I don't want to make everyone's tea taste like egg. Proceed with caution, or follow the instructions on page 44.

Plain Greek yogurt

No sugar or fruit added, please. Go plain (check the ingredients) and add berries or a packet of stevia from your local café for sweetness, if needed. Another confession: I may or may not swipe a couple of extra packets of stevia and throw them in my pocket when I'm buying coffee.

Berries

Great on their own or added to yogurt and oats. Make sure you wash these properly because they've often been sprayed.

Roast chicken

In a pinch, a roast chicken without the stuffing can be a good call. I don't eat the skin, because I don't like the texture.

Canned tuna

Line-caught is a good option if you can find it. I like to buy mine in spring water or brine and add my own good-quality olive oil as a dressing, so I can control the amount. Canned smoked oysters are totally underrated: give them a try.

Jerky

Look for only meat and spices on the ingredients label, as sugar is often added. Let's be clear: sugar isn't the devil, but it does sneak into a lot of packaged foods.

Firm tofu

Another good protein source that doesn't have tons of additives. Skip the silk version because it's wobbly and will probably drip all over your shirt.

Hummus + carrots or celery sticks

Most supermarkets sell pre-cut celery and carrot sticks. Grab some along with a tub of hummus. Hummus should be made with olive oil or no oil. Some brands sneak in less healthy oils, so keep an eye on the ingredients list.

Salad bags

Pick up leaves that are washed and ready to eat. No one wants to see you playing human salad spinner, twirling around the office with your leaves. (Unless you really don't want to keep your job, that is.)

Instant oats packets

Mix them up in a mug with some boiling water if you don't have access to a microwave. Buy the plain ones; flavored versions, like "creamy honey," have added stuff you just don't need. Throw in some berries for sweetness if you like.

I love to add a pinch of stevia and cinnamon

Tip

If you're buying ready-made stuff, I recommend that you learn to read food labels and spot the red herrings. Ideally avoid yucky corn oils, thickeners, additives, e-numbers, flavors, or one of the vast array of added sugars that commercial manufacturers add to foods to make them addictive and cheap to produce. If you see an ingredient you don't like, look for alternative products on the shelf. Top tip: Ingredients are listed in order of volume.

Your Fridge as a Salad Bar

We all love the food-court salad bar: container after container of different pre-cut salad components so you can build your own with all your favorites. You're about to re-create that for yourself at home. Welcome to your new fridge system.

Meal prep is made a thousand times easier if you cut and chop everything and store it in containers ready to grab and go. Not only does it make healthy eating and food assembly that much easier but it also helps ensure you don't leave stuff in the crisper until it's covered in fridge slime weeks later. It also means you get your knife and chopping board out only once, instead of multiple times during the week. It's honestly a game changer. SO . . . here's how to turn your fridge into the best-looking salad bar you've ever seen.

1 Clean out your fridge

Go to your fridge right now (assuming you're at home; don't go poking in other people's) and pull out any rotten fruits and veggies, sauces past their best-by dates, questionable dairy products, and other things you're never going to eat. Toss them out.

2 Go meal-prep shopping

Restock all your favorite fruits and veggies, but only enough for the next five days or they get relegated to the freezer. Flip through this book and, if something catches your eye, work out what you need to make it and what you already have.

3 Prep

As soon as you get home from the store, you're going to prep. There's no point in squeezing it all haphazardly into the fridge and then pulling it all out again. Get out a chopping board and your favorite sharp knife. Grab your spiralizer, too, if you have one. At the same time, grab some storage containers and set them out.

4 Chop

* Halve tomatoes
* Cut corn kernels off the cob
* Chop onions
* Cut carrots into sticks
* Wash celery and cut into hand-length sticks
* Spiralize zucchini
* Wrap herbs in damp paper towels

And so on and so on. You get the idea.

Bonus points: poach chicken breasts (see pages 50–51) and cook grains (see page 89) on the stove while you start chopping. If you have space, you can also prep things like your Perfect Roast Veggies (see page 102), ready to toss into a pan.

5 Store

Pop all your goodies into containers and pack your fridge. Got space for some dressings? Now is a super time to jump on that, too. Grab a jar, turn to pages 122–23, throw in the ingredients for the dressing of your choice, and shake. Store it in the fridge door. Now you have something resembling an EPIC SALAD BAR, ready to pick and choose.

Want a snack? You'll be more tempted to grab a handful of cherry tomatoes or radishes and hummus if everything's already prepped.

Time-saving tip

Don't peel fruits and veggies: the skin adds extra crunch and fiber. Just give them a good rinse in the sink. Ignore this tip for bananas: obviously their skin tastes GROSS.

Prep Your Freezer

Your freezer is where you store partly prepped ingredients and leftover meals. Freeze soups, stews, and pasta sauces in individual containers, ready for quick midweek meals. You'll find plenty to freeze in Step 2, when you're batch-making like a boss, too. Here's what you'll always find in my freezer.

Cheese

I don't eat lots of cheese, but the larger blocks are usually more cost-effective. When I know I won't get through a whole block, I freeze half, or whatever's left, to cut down on waste. It will keep well for about two months. It often gets a bit more crumbly once thawed, but still tastes delish. Tip: Grate it before freezing to speed up the thawing time.

Cream

Again, I don't use that much of this, so any leftover cream goes into ice trays or freezer-safe jars. Sour cream is the exception: this tends to separate when frozen, so use it up or toss it out.

Nuts + seeds

These guys have a high fat content, so they store super-well in the freezer and will last a year or more. What's best is you can eat them straight from the freezer without defrosting— they're just a bit crunchier, which makes them all the more delicious!

Frozen vegetables

If you're in a pinch and forgot to buy veggies on the way home, freezer vegetables will always save you. Buy bags of frozen peas, beans, corn kernels, broccoli, and cauliflower and keep them in the freezer for emergencies. If you're really on the ball, you can chop and blanch your own fresh veggies and freeze them in airtight containers.

Frozen berries

Freeze your own when they're fresh and in season, and they'll be loaded with nutrients when you come to eat them. Great for crumbles, smoothies, baking, or to throw into some plain yogurt for a chilled snack on a summer's day.

Paleo Bread (see pages 90–91)

I always slice and freeze any leftovers, ready to whip up a nutritious snack or meal. Defrost it and lightly toast it to bring back its texture and flavor when you're ready to eat it.

Sliced Chicken Meatloaf (see pages 52–53)

Ready to toast and serve with a spread of avocado, or toss chunks into a salad.

Ice trays with random stuff

I fill ice trays with leftover sauces, hummus, the last of my homemade pesto, citrus juice, and chopped herbs with olive oil. You can wrap these to keep other flavors from permeating them, or buy trays with lids, if you're super-organized.

Ginger

Whole pieces of ginger can be tossed into the freezer in a resealable plastic bag or airtight container. When you want to use some, no need to defrost. Just grate straight into your tea, stir-fry, or dressing. No more fuzzy fridge ginger!

Chopped onion and garlic

Whenever I have these guys going to waste, I freeze them. Toss them into your frying pan straight from the freezer to add flavor to so many dishes.

Smoothie bags (see pages 82–83)

Totally not a new idea, but absolutely worth mentioning as a meal-prep concept. Whenever you have leftover fruits and veggies that have seen better days, chop them up and throw them in a resealable plastic bag. I leave three or four in the freezer and keep adding to them and taking out what I need, when I need it.

Cooked grains

Cook, let them cool, and store them in an airtight container in the freezer. When you're ready to use them, put them in a bowl and reheat in the microwave or add to a saucepan on the stovetop with a splash of water.

Freezer tips

Different zones of your freezer will cool at different rates. When freezing liquid leftovers such as smoothies and soups, put the containers in the coldest part of your freezer (usually the bottom drawer) to increase the speed at which the food is frozen. This prevents the formation of those large ice crystals that give a yucky texture to the defrosted food.

Don't forget that food expands when it freezes, so don't fill containers to the brim. This will avoid messy explosions and broken containers.

Storage Containers

My top piece of advice here is to use containers that you already have and buy new ones or replacements only when you need them. Make sure you have a range of sizes and that they're stackable for easier storage.

I've tried many containers for storing prepped ingredients and leftovers. Some haven't worked well—they don't stack, or they don't keep things fresh—so they've been relegated to the pantry. I now have a few favorites on rotation in the fridge that get used every week to store lunches, snacks, and chopped veggies.

Glass versus plastic

Glass containers are great for keeping things crispy or hard. If you're storing cookies, for example, glass containers will help them keep their crunch. They're usually easier to clean than plastic, and don't stain. They also work well when reheating food, if that's your thing.

Plastic containers, on the other hand, can be lightweight and easy to stack. Look for the ones that are BPA-free. Bonus points if they're also dishwasher and microwave safe.

My personal preference is glass, although it can be heavy to tote to work. Consider whether you commute on foot and are carting your food around—in which case, you're going to love lightweight plastic containers.

I also have a few extras in my food storage system: beeswax fabric wraps for smaller items or to replace missing lids from glass jars (just add a rubber band), and cotton produce bags, a great solution for loose fruit and veggies such as apples, lemons, peppers, etc. They're both reusable and environmentally friendly.

Leakability (not a real word)

Whether you go for plastic or glass, make sure it has an airtight seal. This will keep it from dripping all over your handbag/manbag. (The maker of my favorite pink wallet does NOT know how to get soy sauce off leather—dammit!) If you're clumsy like me, invest in leakproof containers and/or a reusable lunch bag.

Durability

Cheap, thin plastic containers (like the ones you get takeout in) are fine in the fridge, but it's unlikely they'll travel well. For grab-and-go food, make sure you have some stronger options on hand. They'll generally last longer, and price-per-use means they work out to be a better investment.

Size

Life can be so much easier if you have a range of sizes: it means you can save everything from a couple of tablespoons of leftover sauce to an entire meal's worth of veggies.

Recycling

Glass jars are awesome. Next time you finish a jar of olives or honey, clean it well and use it to store snacks, sauces, smoothies, leftover stock, and so on. Jars are durable and FREE! I get a lot of glass containers from secondhand stores and give them a really good wash. Not only are you spending money for a good cause but you're recycling, too. Just be sure to check for any chips or cracks. Clean family-size yogurt tubs can be reused to make and store overnight oats (page 80) and progurt (page 26).

Meal Prep Kitchen Equipment

You don't need fancy gadgets to get started on your meal prep. Keep it simple with the essentials when you're starting out. It's likely you'll already have enough of these to get you up and running. That being said, a well-equipped kitchen is super-helpful and will save you even more time.

Parchment paper and foil
Keeps things from sticking to your pans, and saves dishwashing time, too.

Baking sheets
I always have three of these on hand at any one time, because my oven is usually multitasking on every shelf.

Chef's knife
Great for tough veggies: think pumpkin, raw beets, and sweet potato.

Chopping board
I have an EXTRA LARGE one so I can chop tons of things and pile them up on the same board. Perfect when prepping your fridge as a salad bar, and for everything in between.

Grater (or food processor with grater attachment)
Grate carrots, cheese, and zucchini (if you don't feel like spiralizing).

Ice trays
For freezing cooked mashed veggies, leftover dressings, leftover smoothies, and so on.

Kitchen scissors
Sturdy scissors you'll be using for a million tasks, from trimming chicken breasts to chopping fresh herbs.

Loaf pan
If you have a silicone one, it's super-handy because you don't have to line it with parchment paper, but any nonstick pan will do.

Measuring cups
To measure out liquids, or for making and storing sauces, ready to pour.

Mixing bowls
Grab two—a medium and a large—so you can prep a few things at the same time without hassle.

Serrated knife
Slides through soft fruits and veggies with ease: strawberries, tomatoes, etc.

Silicone spatula

Mix, spread, and even turn things while sautéing. This is an awesome multiuse tool.

Spiralizer

Grab a cheap one if you're feeling lucky, or make an investment in a good one, available in most kitchen equipment stores.

Tongs

To move, grip, and turn food.

Utility or paring knife

Good for chopping smaller things, such as garlic, ginger, and chili.

Whisk

For adding air to ingredients when mixing them together. Hello, light and fluffy!

Zester

Super-useful when adding citrus peel for flavor in savory and sweet dishes. If you don't have one, a cheese grater or some fancy knife skills will do the trick just as well.

Step 1

PREP YOUR PROTEIN

Salmon Gravlax

Portions 10 | **Hands-on prep time** 30 minutes

This no-cook salmon feels like it should be for special occasions only, but it's so simple to make, and freezes well, too. I love mine with the Oaty Seed Crackers (see page 96) and fresh goat cheese.

¾ cup (240 g) rock salt
1 bunch dill, coarsely chopped
zest from 2 organic lemons

2¼ lb (1 kg) fresh salmon fillet,
or 4 skinless salmon fillets

1 Combine the salt, dill, and lemon zest in a bowl.

2 Spread half the mixture over the base of a glass or ceramic dish and lay the salmon on top.

3 Top with the remaining salt mixture.

4 Cover and refrigerate for 24 hours, turning after 12 hours.

5 Remove the salmon from the dish, wash away any loose salt mixture, and pat dry with paper towel.

6 Slice just before eating. Holding a sharp knife at a 45-degree angle, slice the salmon across the grain as thinly as possible.

Save

Salt-cured gravlax can be covered and kept in the fridge for up to twelve days. Freeze whole pieces for up to two months and defrost before slicing.

Foolproof Oven-Baked Salmon

Portions 4 | **Hands-on prep time** 5 minutes

Salmon is so delicious and easy to prep. It's my go-to meal after a long day. You really can't go wrong with this super-simple method for cooking it.

1 Preheat the oven to 350°F.

2 Pat the salmon dry with a paper towel and rub with the olive oil.

3 Place the salmon in a roasting pan, skin-side down. Transfer to the oven.

4 Salmon needs to be cooked for around 4–5 minutes per half inch (1.25 cm) of thickness. Since most fillets are around 1 inch (2.5 cm) at their thickest part, check for doneness at around the 8-minute mark. Fish is cooked when it can be easily flaked with a fork (without the help of a knife to rip it apart).

5 Serve with a sprinkling of sea salt flakes, freshly ground black pepper, and some sprigs of dill or basil, if using.

That salt + fat combo is SO GOOD

4 salmon fillets, skin on
2 tablespoons olive oil
2 teaspoons sea salt flakes
Freshly ground black pepper
Dill and basil sprigs, to serve
  (optional)

Save

Keep leftover fillets refrigerated for up to five days. They can be gently reheated or eaten cold.

Tip

I totally urge you to try salmon medium-rare. My mom crucified it for years, not knowing that you can eat good-quality salmon totally raw. Now I'm the biggest lover of the flavorful, super-soft pink flesh in the middle: a much more delicious mouth feel, and the flavor is more delicate.

Sugar-free teriyaki glaze

Mix together 3 tablespoons soy sauce or tamari + 2 teaspoons sesame oil + 1 teaspoon freshly grated ginger + 1 tablespoon dijon mustard + 10 drops liquid stevia. Before baking, baste the salmon and sprinkle with 1 tablespoon of sesame seeds.

Meal-Prepped Eggs 101

These nutrition powerhouses are great ready-to-eat snacks, and are delicious added to a veggie dish for a protein boost. You can cook them in advance and store them in the fridge. WIN!

Boiled

Everyone has their own way of boiling eggs. Some begin with a pan of cold water, but I'm all about speed when it comes to meal prep. If you're anything like me, you love your whites set but your yolk gooey. For convenience's sake, I don't want to bite into an egg and have yolk running down my face (that has TOTALLY happened to me), so I've perfected the gooey yolk without the drip factor.

Put water in a saucepan and bring to a simmer. Reduce heat to medium, then lower in eggs (gently—no cracked shells if possible!) and immediately set the timer on your phone for 6 minutes. When the time is up, tip out the hot water and run cold water over the eggs for a few minutes to stop them from cooking further. Allow to cool completely before storing them in a bowl in the fridge or back in the carton. Be sure to write "BOILED" on the carton to avoid eggcidents.

4 minutes—very runny
6 minutes—gooey
8 minutes—thick
10 minutes—hard-boiled

Good for slicing and grating over stuff

4 mins   6 mins   8 mins   10 mins

Tip

Fresher eggs are harder to peel, so use older eggs for boiling. Only peel boiled eggs when you're ready to eat them; they'll keep for longer with the shells on.

Poached

You can prep your favorite poached eggs up to five days before eating, and store them in the fridge.

To start, break a very fresh egg into a sieve and swirl it a little to remove any watery white, then pop it into a bowl. This keeps the whites from doing that foamy thing all over your pan. Repeat with up to five more eggs (this will work with a medium-to-large pan; do a few less if you only have a small one).

Tip the eggs slowly into a pan of simmering water, ideally one at a time. Don't worry—as long as the yolks haven't broken, they won't stick together into one very large egg (though that could be kind of awesome). When they've been in the hot water for around 15 seconds, stir gently to distribute the eggs around the pan. After 3–4 minutes, the egg whites will be set and the yolks still gooey. Using a slotted spoon, carefully remove the eggs one by one and pop them into a container filled with cold water—a few ice cubes can help stop the cooking process.

To reheat the eggs without overcooking them, fill a bowl with hot water (from your tap, not boiling) and lower in the eggs you're about to serve. Leave them to warm up for 2 minutes, then remove with a slotted spoon and serve.

A one-quart mason jar is the perfect size to hold a dozen eggs

Pickled

Okay, you might associate pickled eggs with pub food, but they're delicious and an awesome way of making something nutritious and versatile in batches. Plus they keep in the fridge FOREVER. In other words, these bad boys are meal-prep VIPs.

The more you can pickle at once, the less time spent cooking in the future. I recommend doing a full dozen and getting your hands on a huge jar for this one.

To make pickled eggs, boil the eggs in the shell for a full 10 minutes. When they're cool, peel off the shells.

In a saucepan over medium-high heat, bring all of the remaining ingredients to a boil, then reduce the heat and simmer for 5 minutes.

Remove from the heat and allow the vinegar mixture to cool slightly. Put the eggs into a sterilized jar and pour the vinegar mixture over the top until the jar is full and all the eggs are completely covered. Allow to cool completely before putting on the lid and refrigerating for up to four months.

You can enjoy these just a few days after pickling, but they taste EXTRA after a week or two.

Ingredients

12 eggs
½ teaspoon mustard seeds
1½ cups (375 ml) white or
   apple cider vinegar
¾ cup (185 ml) water
2 teaspoons sea salt
2 sprigs fresh tarragon
1 garlic clove, quartered

love garlic? Add a few extra cloves

Save

These last three to four months in the fridge.

One-Tray Chicken: Three Ways

Portions 6 | **Hands-on prep time** 10 minutes

When you're rotating lean meats such as chicken for a lot of meals, dinner can get pretty tedious. This simple hack lets you cook chicken three different ways in one tray. I'm all about multitasking! Use foil to create dividing walls in your pan so you can season each portion differently. Use your fave seasonings or try mine.

3 large skinless chicken breasts
2 tablespoons olive oil
1 teaspoon each salt + pepper

1 tablespoon each of seasonings, opposite

1 Preheat the oven to 350°F.

2 Using a pair of kitchen scissors, trim off any white sinew from the meat, then cut it into ¾ inch (2 cm) pieces.

3 Lay an extra-large piece of foil on a baking sheet, spread out the chicken, and drizzle with olive oil. Season with salt and pepper.

4 Divide the chicken evenly into three portions, and pinch two "walls" in the foil to create separate sections, as shown.

5 Season each section with a different seasoning mixture, rub into the chicken, and bake for 10–15 minutes or until cooked through.

Save

Keep the cooked chicken in separate airtight containers in the fridge for up to four days.

My top three chicken seasonings

Spicy barbecue

Smoked paprika + garlic
powder + onion powder +
chili powder

Maple sesame

1 tablespoon maple syrup
+ 2 tablespoons sesame
seeds + 1 teaspoon garlic
powder + 1 teaspoon
ground ginger

Lemon + rosemary

Lemon zest + lemon juice
+ finely chopped fresh
rosemary

Milk-Poached Chicken

Serves 4 | **Hands-on prep time** 10 minutes

Poached chicken offers a deliciously consistent moist texture, and takes less time than you'd think. The milk captures the flavors and can be reserved and used as a soup base (see opposite).

3 cups (750 ml) milk (I use unsweetened almond milk)
4 garlic cloves or 2 teaspoons garlic powder

10 peppercorns
Fresh tarragon (optional)
4 skinless, boneless chicken breasts

1   Heat the milk in a saucepan over medium heat, together with the garlic, peppercorns, and tarragon (if using), until just simmering.

2   Lower the chicken breasts into the poaching liquid and set a timer for 15–20 minutes, depending on their size.

3   Remove the chicken from the poaching liquid and set aside.

4   Allow to cool before slicing or shredding the chicken into long strands with your hands.

Save

Store in an airtight container in the fridge for up to four days.

Tip

You can poach chicken in the same amount of stock, or plain old water, if you're trying to keep it super simple. Same method and cooking times apply.

(+ soup with the leftovers)

Soup

Reserve the poaching liquid for soup: throw in 1½ cups of your oldest veggies (I usually have extra celery and leeks) and simmer for 15 minutes. If you want extra flavor, add a chicken stock cube. Blend until smooth, with a good dollop of mustard if you like. Cool and store in the fridge; it will be good for two to three days. You can freeze it in single-serving portions, too.

Basic Chicken Meatloaf ← *Slice + freeze*

Portions 8 | **Hands-on prep time** 10 minutes

Slice meatloaf into single-serving portions before freezing and
defrost at room temp whenever you want a satisfying protein punch.

1   Preheat the oven to 350°F.

2   Put all of the ingredients into a bowl and use your hands to mix
until well combined.

3   Press the mixture into a silicone loaf pan (or a loaf pan lined
with parchment paper) and bake for 40–45 minutes until cooked
through. Set aside for 10 minutes before removing from the pan
and slicing.

4   You can also spoon the mixture into a muffin pan to cook
individual portions.

1 lb (500 g) ground chicken
1½ cups grated vegetables*
4 eggs
3 tablespoons Caramelized Onions
(see page 104) or 1 medium onion,
chopped
1½ teaspoons finely chopped garlic
(or 1 teaspoon garlic powder)
1 tablespoon Worcestershire sauce
(see opposite for flavor bomb
substitutions)
½ teaspoon sea salt flakes
Freshly ground black pepper

** I love zucchini
and carrot*

Save

Freeze the slices
between sheets of
parchment paper
for up to one month.
Store in an airtight
container in the fridge
for up to four days.

Flavor bombs

Replace Worcestershire
sauce with any one of
these options:

* chopped fresh cilantro
* 1 tablespoon mustard
* 1 tablespoon chili flakes
* 1 tablespoon miso paste
* 1 tablespoon sriracha

Nut Butter Falafel

Makes about 18 | **Hands-on prep time** 20 minutes

Chickpeas and nut butter are great vegetarian protein options. Add your favorite flavor combo from the options below or invent your own.

1 Preheat the oven to 350°F.

2 Mix all of the ingredients together in a blender or food processor until they're well combined.

3 Add your choice of flavors to the mixture in the blender (see below for some suggestions).

4 Roll the mixture into balls with your hands. If the dough is a little wet, add more almond meal or flour, a little at a time.

5 Place the balls on a silicone baking sheet or a baking sheet lined with parchment paper. Bake for 20 minutes or until golden brown.

14 oz (400 g) can chickpeas, drained and rinsed
½ cup chopped cooked pumpkin (see page 100)
½ cup (50 g) almond meal or other flour
1 teaspoon baking powder
3 tablespoons natural peanut butter
1 tablespoon lemon juice

Almond butter and tahini also work—whatever you have in the cupboard is fine

Save

Store in the fridge for five days, or freeze for up to two weeks.

My top three flavor combos

Traditional

2 teaspoons cumin
+ 1 teaspoon allspice
+ 1 teaspoon onion powder

Moroccan

2 teaspoons turmeric
+ 1 teaspoon garam masala
+ 1 teaspoon garlic powder

Green goodness

½ bunch fresh basil
+ ½ bunch fresh mint
+ 2 tablespoons pine nuts

Cauliflower Steaks

Portions 4 | **Hands-on prep time** 10 minutes

Slice a cauliflower into thick "steaks." Save any rogue florets to make vegetable rice, or toss them into smoothie bags (see pages 82–83).

1 Preheat the oven to 350°F.

2 Remove the large outer leaves from the cauliflower (leaving some on is fine) and trim the stalk.

3 Slice lengthwise through the center to produce four ¾ inch (2 cm) thick "steaks."

4 Lay the steaks on a baking sheet lined with parchment paper. Drizzle with olive oil and flip over to coat both sides.

5 Sprinkle with salt, pepper, and any herbs or spices you like.

6 Roast for 25–30 minutes until golden and tender.

1 large head of cauliflower
Olive oil
1 tablespoon of your favorite herb
  or spice mixture

Make

Make these at the same time as your Perfect Roast Veggies (see page 102).

Save

Store in the fridge, covered, for up to three days.

Tip

These work well as a toast substitute for breakfast. Top with sliced avocado and a poached egg (see page 45) for a super-quick nutritious start to the day.

Indian twist

Add curry powder and garam masala before roasting and serve with plain yogurt, a handful of raisins, and some fresh cilantro for a delicious veggie dish!

Miso Eggplant

Portions 4 | **Hands-on prep time** 10 minutes

Add a little Japanese flavor to your busy weekdays with this simple miso eggplant. While eggplant isn't technically a protein, it's often the star of a vegetarian dinner plate.

2 eggplants
Olive oil cooking spray
1 tablespoon miso paste
1½ tablespoons soy sauce
  or tamari

1 inch (3 cm) piece of fresh ginger,
  grated
2 large garlic cloves, finely chopped
1 teaspoon coconut sugar
Black sesame seeds, to serve

1   Preheat the oven to 350°F.

2   Using a sharp knife, cut the eggplants lengthways down the middle.

3   Now score the eggplant diagonally one way then the other to create a crosshatch effect. Spray or drizzle with a little olive oil and bake for 20 minutes.

4   Meanwhile, create the glaze by mixing the miso paste with tamari, ginger, garlic, coconut sugar, and ¼ cup (60 ml) of water in a small saucepan over high heat.

5   Boil the miso mixture until thickened and brush it over the flesh of the eggplant. Bake for a further 5–10 minutes until caramelized, then remove from the oven. Allow to cool for 5 minutes before serving, sprinkled with the sesame seeds.

Save

Unused portions can be stored in the fridge for up to three days.

Lemon-Broiled Striped Bass

Portions 4 | **Hands-on prep time** 10 minutes

This recipe works well with any white-fleshed fish. Try it with mahi-mahi, catfish, tilapia, or whatever is on sale at the fishmonger. It makes an awesome addition to salad or tacos.

1 Preheat the broiler on high.

2 Lay the fish in a glass dish or on a baking sheet lined with parchment paper and drizzle with olive oil.

3 Grate the zest from the lemon and sprinkle it over the fish, then squeeze half the lemon juice over and sprinkle with garlic powder. Thinly slice the remaining lemon half and lay over the top of the fish.

4 Scatter the scallions and parsley (if using) over the top.

5 Broil for 15-20 minutes until the fish is cooked through and flakes with a fork. Serve scattered with herbs.

4 striped bass fillets (approximately 7 oz or 200 g each) or 1 whole fish (approximately 2¼ lb or 1 kg)
2 tablespoons olive oil
1 large lemon
1 teaspoon garlic powder
¼ cup sliced scallions
2 tablespoons chopped fresh parsley (optional)
Fresh herbs, to serve

Make

Before cooking, prep the fish and freeze in portions. You can defrost a portion in the fridge before broiling.

Save

Cooked fish can be stored in the freezer for up to a month. Store leftovers in the refrigerator overnight.

Tip

Many lemons from the supermarket are waxed. Avoid getting wax all over your fish by pouring boiling water over the lemon in your kitchen sink. Give it a quick scrub with a veggie brush to remove any residue.

Healthy Fish Cakes

Portions 4 | **Hands-on prep time** 15 minutes

These fish cakes can be made kid-friendly by shaping them into fingers and coating with rice flour instead of sesame seeds. Use the same weight of canned tuna or salmon if you don't have fresh fish.

1 Preheat the oven to 350°F.

2 Throw everything (aside from the sesame seeds) into a blender or food processor and blitz to a coarse consistency.

3 Use wet hands to roll the mixture into patties, then dip into the sesame seeds to coat.

4 Bake for 15-20 minutes until cooked through, or pan-fry in a little oil (sesame oil is YUM) for 3-4 minutes on each side.

1 lb (500 g) fresh white-fleshed fish, coarsely chopped
1 small onion, chopped
1 garlic clove (or ½ teaspoon garlic powder)
½ bunch fresh parsley (stalks and all!)
Juice of ½ lemon
Sea salt + pepper
½ cup (75 g) sesame seeds
Sesame oil, for frying (optional)

I love these served with salad and Coconut Tzatziki (see page 123)

Save

Freeze uncooked patties, before dipping them in the sesame seeds, in an airtight container for up to three months.

Tip

If you don't have a food processor, just chop everything up reaaaaally finely.

Make them Thai-style

* ½ inch (1 cm) piece of fresh ginger, grated, or 1 teaspoon ground ginger
* use lime instead of lemon
* use cilantro instead of parsley
* 1 tablespoon soy sauce or tamari

Satay Tofu Crumble

Portions 4 | **Hands-on prep time** 10 minutes

Tofu gets a bad rap for being bland, but pump up the flavor and it's something to daydream about (don't pretend you don't think about dinner at work). This version is a 10 out of 10 on the flavor scale.

1   Cut tofu into ½ inch (1 cm) thick slices and lay them in a single layer on a plate lined with a paper towel. Cover with more paper towels and press down firmly to squeeze out any excess liquid.

2   Heat 1 tablespoon of sesame oil in a large frying pan. Cook the tofu slices for 7–10 minutes until browned on both sides. Transfer to a plate to cool.

3   Meanwhile, whisk together the soy sauce, lime juice, sriracha, peanut butter, ginger, and remaining sesame oil in a medium bowl.

4   Crumble the tofu into small pieces and add to the bowl with the sauce. Toss to combine.

1 lb (500 g) firm tofu
2 tablespoons sesame oil
3 tablespoons soy sauce or tamari
2 tablespoons lime juice
1 tablespoon sriracha
5 teaspoons natural crunchy
   peanut butter
1 teaspoon freshly grated ginger
   (or ground equivalent)
Basil leaves and crushed peanuts,
   to serve

Save

Satay tofu crumble can be kept, covered, in the fridge for up to five days.

Smoky Turkey Rissoles

Portions 3-4 | **Hands-on prep time** 15 minutes

Enjoy three of these rissoles as part of a main meal, or snack
on a couple for a protein kick any time of day.

1 Preheat the oven to 350°F.

2 Put the turkey, spices, and salt in a bowl and use your hands to
combine well.

3 Grab a palm-sized amount of mixture and roll it into a ball,
or press lightly into patties if you prefer.

4 Place on a baking sheet lined with parchment paper and repeat
with the remaining mixture to make about 9 balls or patties.

5 Bake for 15–20 minutes until beginning to brown on top.

6 Remove from the oven and allow to cool. Serve with micro herbs
and extra chili flakes, if you like.

1 lb (500 g) ground turkey
1 teaspoon garlic powder
1 teaspoon smoked paprika
1 teaspoon chili flakes (optional)
1 teaspoon sea salt flakes (use
  smoked salt if you have it!)
Micro herbs and extra chili flakes,
  to serve (optional)

Dunk in green dressing (see page 123)

Save

Store in the fridge
for up to four days,
or freeze for up to
two months.

Asian-Style Ground Turkey

Portions 4 | **Hands-on prep time** 5 minutes

This spicy dish is super-versatile for midweek meals and freezes really well. Always defrost and reheat on the same day, making sure it's piping hot.

1 Heat the peanut oil in a frying pan over medium-high heat.

2 Add the ground turkey, garlic, and chili, cooking for 4–5 minutes, stirring regularly, until cooked through.

3 Add the soy, lime, and stevia or honey in the final minute of cooking. Stir well to coat the meat, then remove from heat.

4 Scatter with cilantro and fresh chili. Serve with lime wedges, if you like.

2 tablespoons peanut oil

1 lb (500 g) lean ground turkey

2 garlic cloves, crushed, or
   1 teaspoon garlic powder

1 red chili, thinly sliced, or
   1 tablespoon dried chili flakes

3 tablespoons soy sauce or tamari

Zest and juice of 1 lime

½ tablespoon granulated stevia or
   1 tablespoon honey

Fresh cilantro, sliced red chili, and
   lime wedges, to serve (optional)

Save

Allow cooked turkey to cool before storing in an airtight container in the fridge for three to four days, or for two months in the freezer.

Spicy Ground Bison

Portions 4 | **Hands-on prep time** 10 minutes

Bison is a lean meat with a high iron and zinc content, so it makes an interesting alternative to other red meats. No bison? This recipe works well with beef, too.

1 Heat the oil in a frying pan over medium heat. Add the garlic, cooking for 1 minute.

2 Add the ground bison and scallions, chili flakes, cumin, and cayenne. Mix well and cook for 5 minutes, stirring regularly, until cooked through.

3 Serve with cilantro and extra scallions.

½ tablespoon olive oil or coconut oil

2 garlic cloves, finely chopped

1 lb (500 g) lean ground bison or beef

½ cup chopped scallions, plus extra to serve

1 tablespoon chili flakes

1 teaspoon ground cumin

1 teaspoon cayenne pepper

Fresh cilantro, to serve

I keep chopped scallions in a container in the fridge, ready to scatter over dishes like this

Save

Allow cooked bison to cool before storing in an airtight container in the fridge for three to four days, or for two months in the freezer.

Chicken Crust Meatza

Portions 4 | **Hands-on prep time** 15 minutes

This pizza is great for gluten-free, paleo, and keto diets. I love a few slices with a big salad.

1 Preheat a broiler on high.

2 Put the chicken, flour, nutritional yeast (if using), garlic, onion, and salt in a large bowl. Mix well (I just repeatedly squeeze it between my hands) and spread on a baking sheet lined with parchment paper. Loosely squish so you can lay another piece of parchment paper over the top.

3 Use a rolling pin (or the roll of parchment paper with elastic bands or hair ties on the ends to keep it from unraveling) to roll out the mixture to about ¼ inch (5 mm) thick. Shape it into a rectangle for easier freezing.

4 Peel back the top layer of parchment paper and broil for 10–12 minutes until the meat is cooked through and starting to brown on the edges.

5 Remove from under the broiler and spread with the purée or pesto. Add toppings (see below), then return to the broiler for 5–10 minutes until the toppings are warm and cheese has melted.

6 Remove from the broiler and slice to serve. Leftover topped slices can be kept in the fridge for up to three days.

1 lb (500 g) lean ground chicken
2 tablespoons coconut flour
¼ cup nutritional yeast (optional)
1 teaspoon garlic powder
1 teaspoon onion powder
1 teaspoon sea salt
½ cup (125 ml) tomato purée
  or pesto

Enjoy leftovers cold! There's nothing like cold meatza for breakfast.

 Make
Topping ideas:
Perfect Roast Veggies
  (see page 102)
Sliced tomato
Anchovies
Sliced onion
Cheese: mozzarella,
  cheddar, feta

 Save
Double this recipe and, after the extra crust is broiled, cover and freeze it (without toppings) for up to two months. You can pull it out, dress it, and bake for around 25 minutes at 350°F.

 Tip
I did half-and-half with my toppings. Great option if you're trying to appeal to many tastes! You can sub ground turkey for the chicken, if preferred.

Sweet Potatoes with Baked Eggs

Portions 4 | **Hands-on prep time** 15 minutes

You've probably seen eggs baked in avocado ALL over Instagram (are you following @thefitfoodieblog?). It's a legit delicious snack. This version is all about healthy complex carbs to keep you fueled through the day.

1 Preheat the oven to 350°F. Wash the sweet potatoes and stab them all over with a fork.

2 Microwave for 7–8 minutes. If you prefer, you can bake them (but think of the time you'll save!).

3 Cut the cooked potatoes in half and scoop out about a third of the soft flesh from the center. Reserve the cooked potato to stir into your overnight oats (see page 80), or mash with miso and serve with fish.

4 Place the halves cut-side up on a baking sheet lined with parchment paper. Divide the chopped spinach between the potato halves and crack an egg into each one.

5 Bake for 8–12 minutes, depending on how you like your eggs.

2 large sweet potatoes
½ cup chopped spinach
4 eggs
Julienned radishes and freshly ground black pepper, to serve (optional)

Try chopped onions or peppers instead of spinach

Save

Store the baked potatoes in an airtight container in the fridge for up to two days. If you want to store them for longer, make the potatoes up to step 3 and store in the fridge for up to four days.

Tip

Get creative with toppings! I love scallions, radishes, and black pepper, plus any dressing I have lying around. You should have plenty now that you've made the delish ones from pages 122–23.

Step 2

BATCH AND STASH

DIY Muesli

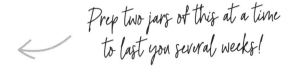
Prep two jars of this at a time to last you several weeks!

GRAINS (5 cups total, any combination)

Rye flakes   Rolled oats   Barley flakes

+

YOUR CHOICE OF CHOPPED NUTS (1 cup total)

Brazil nuts   Almonds   Walnuts   Cashews   Peanuts

+

EXTRA CRUNCH FACTOR (1 cup total)

Sunflower seeds   Pumpkin seeds   Buckwheat groats   Coconut flakes   Cacao nibs   Freeze-dried banana

+

DRIED FRUIT (½ cup, optional)

Raisins   Goji berries   Blueberries   Mulberries   Raspberries

+

FLAVOR BOMBS (½ teaspoon)

Ground cardamom   Ground cinnamon   Sea salt   Ground vanilla

= quickest breakfast ever!

Soak
Add 1 cup milk and leave for a few hours. Kinda like Overnight Oats (see page 80).

Heat
Put ¾ cup muesli and ½ cup (125 ml) milk in a small saucepan and cook for 10 minutes over medium heat, stirring regularly.

Toast
Add 3 tablespoons honey or your favorite sweetener and 2 tablespoons melted coconut oil to the mix before adding any dried fruit. Stir to coat and spread onto a lined baking sheet. Toast in a preheated oven at 350°F for 15–20 minutes until golden brown. Allow to cool and stir in the fruit.

Top
Scatter muesli over plain Greek yogurt and add fresh berries for a simple and tasty breakfast.

Five Days of Overnight Oats

Portions 5 | **Hands-on prep time** 10 minutes

Prepping oats in big batches for the week ahead is a surefire way of saving yourself from the bagel cart at work. The fiber takes a while to digest, so these keep you full for longer (use rolled oats rather than quick ones, as they take longer for your body to break down). Not a whiz in the kitchen? If I was to offer one recipe to someone with zero cooking ability who was trying to eat healthily, this would be it. Ten minutes' investment equals a nutritious start to the day for five days. What a payoff! Do you prefer sweet or savory?

Watch out for the high sodium content of some ready-made stock

Sweet

5 cups (500 g) rolled oats
¼ cup (40 g) chia seeds
5 cups (1.25 liters) milk of your choice
1 teaspoon vanilla extract or ground vanilla

Savory

5 cups (500 g) rolled oats
¼ cup (40 g) chia seeds
5 cups (1.25 liters) water or leftover Milk-Poached Chicken stock (see page 50) or vegetable stock
½ teaspoon sea salt

Mix all of the ingredients together in a bowl, cover, and leave to soak in the fridge. Spoon portions into small, portable jars or airtight containers and top with your fave topping combos when you're ready to eat them.

Sweet topping combos

* Walnuts + ½ cup grated carrot + nutmeg + 1 teaspoon honey
* Sliced banana + peanut butter + cinnamon
* Cocoa powder + raspberries + toasted coconut + cacao nibs
* DIY Trail Mix (see page 126) + sliced strawberries + 2 squares dark chocolate

Savory topping combos

* Poached Egg (see page 45) + avocado + turkey bacon
* ½ teaspoon chili flakes + 1 teaspoon tamari or soy sauce + cilantro + Poached Chicken (see page 50)
* Canned sardines + grated zucchini + lemon juice + pepper
* Miso pumpkin mash + chopped Thai basil + cashews

Tip *Sweet*

Add a few tablespoons of this to smoothies before blending for extra fiber and creaminess!

Tip *Savory*

Spoon into your soup base before blending to make it thick and super-satisfying.

DIY Smoothie Bags

Smoothie bags are a way to save odds and ends of food in the freezer until you're ready to fire up the blender for a delicious and healthy drink. You can chop and freeze any ingredient you might use in a smoothie, using a resealable plastic bag so that you can easily take out as much as you need at a time.

If you want to be a bit more organized, you can portion the ingredients out, ready to blend first thing in the morning so you can run out the door fast. If you don't have leftovers (who are you?), you can always find some delicious options in the freezer section of the supermarket.

Want to cut the disposable plastic? I use my resealable bags over and over. Give them a wipe with a clean cloth every now and again. Freezer-safe mason jars or containers work, too.

Save

I like to freeze leftover smoothies in ice trays or popsicle molds. They'll last three months in the freezer, so the only thing that might pause your prep is freezer space!

Tip

Freeze a smoothie in a freezer-safe jar or container. Grab the container as you leave the house in the morning and it will be defrosted in time for lunch; or leave it to defrost in the fridge overnight and have it for breakfast.

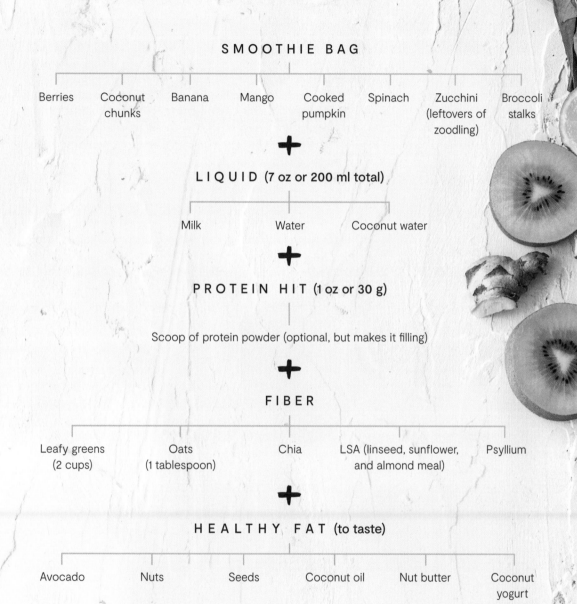

SMOOTHIE BAG

Berries • Coconut chunks • Banana • Mango • Cooked pumpkin • Spinach • Zucchini (leftovers of zoodling) • Broccoli stalks

+

LIQUID (7 oz or 200 ml total)

Milk • Water • Coconut water

+

PROTEIN HIT (1 oz or 30 g)

Scoop of protein powder (optional, but makes it filling)

+

FIBER

Leafy greens (2 cups) • Oats (1 tablespoon) • Chia • LSA (linseed, sunflower, and almond meal) • Psyllium

+

HEALTHY FAT (to taste)

Avocado • Nuts • Seeds • Coconut oil • Nut butter • Coconut yogurt

= perfect smoothie every time!

Smoky Chocolate Cereal Bars

Portions 14 | **Hands-on prep time** 15 minutes

I love a muesli bar as much as the next person, but the ones on supermarket shelves often have a number of suspicious ingredients. Try making a batch of these cereal bars instead. Use plain almonds and salt if you prefer them without the smoky flavor.

2 tablespoons coconut oil

1 cup (200 g) pitted prunes, finely chopped

⅔ cup (180 g) natural peanut or almond butter

1 tablespoon honey or maple syrup

1 cup (160 g) smoked almonds, coarsely chopped

1 cup (30 g) puffed brown rice

¼ cup (30 g) cacao nibs

¼ cup (40 g) pumpkin seeds

5½ oz (150 g) dark chocolate (85% cacao), melted

1 teaspoon smoked sea salt

1 Put the coconut oil and prunes in a large, wide-based saucepan over low to medium heat and mash with a fork.

2 Stir in the nut butter and honey until well combined and gooey.

3 Remove from the heat and stir through almonds, puffed rice, cacao nibs, and pumpkin seeds. Mix well.

4 Press the mixture in a layer about ½ inch (1.5 cm) thick into the base of a silicone baking pan or a baking pan lined with parchment paper.

5 Pour the melted chocolate over and sprinkle with sea salt.

6 Refrigerate until set (about an hour), then slice into bars.

Enjoy licking this bowl!

Save

Refrigerate for up to one week; freeze for three weeks.

DIY Hummus

Portions 10 | **Hands-on prep time** 10 minutes

Everyone needs a great hummus recipe . . . or four. All of the variations here offer a good dose of fiber (which is great for a healthy digestive tract) and pack a punch in the flavor department.

1 Put all of the ingredients into the bowl of a food processor fitted with an S-blade.

2 Process until smooth, stopping to scrape down the sides of the bowl as needed.

1 can of your favorite beans or legumes, drained and rinsed (see options below)

1 garlic clove (or ½ teaspoon garlic powder)

3 tablespoons olive oil

4 tablespoons tahini

2 tablespoons lemon juice

Sea salt + pepper

My favorite combos

At its heart, hummus is simply beans blended with tahini, olive oil, garlic, and lemon. I love these combos.

* lentils + 2 handfuls spinach leaves
* white beans + 1 teaspoon ground cumin
* chickpeas + 1 teaspoon paprika
* black beans + ¼ teaspoon cayenne or chili

Save

Store in a glass jar in the fridge for up to one week. Freeze in an airtight container (with space at the top to leave room for expansion) for six months. Thaw in the refrigerator the day before you want to use it. You can also freeze small portions in an ice tray.

White beans + cumin

Black beans + cayenne

Chickpeas + paprika

Lentils + spinach

Brown rice

Buckwheat

Teff

Freekeh

Supergrains

Portions 8 | **Hands-on prep time** 5 minutes

These grains add new and interesting flavors to any meal, and are less refined than standard white rice. They come with their natural bran and germ, offering you a complete package of nutrition.

1 Put 1 cup of your choice of dry grains (brown rice, buckwheat, teff, freekeh, quinoa, or kamut) in a saucepan and cover with 4 cups (1 liter) of water or stock. A pinch of salt is optional. Bring to a boil, then reduce heat to low, stirring occasionally until the liquid is almost all absorbed and the grain is tender. See approximate cooking times at right.

2 Use a fine sieve for draining so that small grains don't fall through the holes. Set aside to cool before transferring the cooked grains to an airtight container.

Quinoa

Growing grains

1 cup BROWN RICE
+ 50 minutes cooking time
= 2 cups cooked

1 cup BUCKWHEAT
+ 20 minutes cooking time
= 2 cups cooked

1 cup TEFF
+ 20 minutes cooking time
= 3 cups cooked

1 cup FREEKEH
+ 15 minutes cooking time
= 3 cups cooked

1 cup QUINOA
+ 20 minutes cooking time
= 2 cups cooked

1 cup KAMUT
+ 1 hour 30 minutes
  cooking time
= 3 cups cooked

Make

Freeze cooked grains in portions in resealable bags; when you need them for a meal, empty the grains into a bowl of warm water for fifteen minutes to defrost, or put them on the stovetop with a splash of water to heat through.

Save

Cooked grains will last three to four days in the fridge, or two months in the freezer.

Tip

Teff doesn't freeze well, so cook that one as you need it.

I eat mine with a smear of goat cheese, drizzled with olive oil and balsamic glaze

Olive + oregano

One-Bowl Nutty Paleo Bread

Makes 3 loaves | **Hands-on prep time** 20 minutes

You probably don't want to make bread all that often, because it's a laborious process. It's SO much faster to walk to the corner store—I get it. This recipe is nutritious and unlike any other bread you've tasted, so it's worth the effort. It also makes enough for three loaves, so you only have to measure and mix once every few months. YAY!

Mix together the dry ingredients, at right, and store them in an airtight container in your pantry for when that bread craving hits. Feel free to experiment with your own flavor combos: you can even try something a little sweet!

Dry ingredients

3 cups (360 g) golden flaxseed meal

1½ cups (170 g) almond meal

1 cup (120 g) coconut flour

6 tablespoons baking powder

1½ cups (210 g) chopped hazelnuts

1½ cups (220 g) sesame seeds

1½ cups (220 g) sunflower seeds

3 teaspoons sea salt

Rosemary + garlic

Pesto swirl

1 Pick out a flavor variation below. Preheat the oven to 350°F.

2 Weigh out one-third of the dry-ingredient mixture and put it in a bowl, along with your flavor choice. Make a well in the center and crack in 5 lightly beaten eggs. Add 3 tablespoons of liquid coconut oil (not hot, or it will scramble the eggs) and mix well. Spoon the batter into a 9 x 5 inch loaf pan sprayed with cooking spray (or a loaf pan lined with parchment paper) and bake for 35–40 minutes, until a knife inserted in the center comes out clean.

3 Allow the bread to cool before removing it from the pan and storing or slicing.

Save

Store bread in an airtight container for up to five days. Slice before freezing for four months: pop a frozen slice in the toaster for quick and easy toast!

Flavor variations

Olive + oregano

+ ½ cup (60 g) pitted olives + 1 tablespoon dried oregano

Rosemary + garlic

+ 1 tablespoon chopped fresh rosemary leaves + 1½ teaspoons garlic powder

Pesto swirl

+ 3 tablespoons pesto (ready-made is fine) or make your own (see page 122) and swirl through the mixture in the loaf pan before baking

Flax Waffles

Portions 8 | **Hands-on prep time** 10 minutes

Do you prefer sweet or savory waffles? This mixture has you covered for both. You can even split the batter and make half and half.

1 Heat a waffle iron.

2 Put the eggs and oil into a blender with ½ cup (125 ml) of water, blending until foamy.

3 Pour the liquid into a bowl containing the flaxseed meal, baking powder, and salt.

4 Fold the mixture together and leave it in the bowl for 3 minutes.

5 Add herbs or cinnamon.

6 Spoon the mixture onto the hot waffle iron, cook, and repeat until you've cooked all of the mixture.

5 large eggs
⅓ cup (80 ml) extra virgin olive oil or melted coconut oil
2 cups (240 g) golden flaxseed meal
1 tablespoon baking powder
1 teaspoon sea salt
1 tablespoon dried herbs (for savory waffles) or 2 teaspoons ground cinnamon (for sweet)

Save

Freeze cooked waffles between sheets of parchment paper in an airtight container for up to six weeks. Pop straight into the toaster to defrost.

Rosemary and Tahini Cookies

Portions 12 | **Hands-on prep time** 20 minutes

Savory cookies? I promise you won't be disappointed! If there was only one recipe in this book I would urge everyone to try, it would be this one.

1 Preheat the oven to 325°F. Line a baking sheet with parchment paper and set aside.

2 Put the tahini and maple syrup in a small saucepan over low heat and melt them together. Add 1 teaspoon of the salt and stir well, then remove from heat.

3 Mix the almond meal with 1 tablespoon of rosemary in a bowl and stir in the hot tahini mixture. Chill the mixture for 15 minutes.

4 Roll the mixture into 12 balls and set them out on the baking sheet. Press the balls down with the back of a fork and sprinkle with the pistachios, and the remaining rosemary and salt.

5 Bake for 12–14 minutes or until starting to lightly brown. Remove from the oven and let cool on the baking sheet for 10 minutes before transferring to a wire rack to cool completely before storing.

1 cup (270 g) tahini (I used black)
2 tablespoons maple syrup
2 teaspoons sea salt
1¼ cups (125 g) almond meal
2 tablespoons chopped fresh rosemary
1 tablespoon chopped pistachios

Save

Store in an airtight container at room temperature for up to one week. Freeze for up to one month.

Oaty Seed Crackers

Makes 30 | **Hands-on prep time** 25 minutes

Creating a balanced meal is as much about texture as it is flavor balance and those all-important proteins, fats, and carbs. These delicious oaty crackers will add crunch to any meal and are easily packable for a healthy workday snack, too.

1 Preheat the oven to 350°F.

2 In a bowl, mix all of the ingredients together with 1 cup (250 ml) of water and set aside for 15 minutes for the water to soak in.

3 Take a third of the mixture (1½ cups) and roll it out very thin between two sheets of parchment paper on a baking sheet. Repeat to roll out the remaining mixture on two other sheets.

4 Remove the top sheet of parchment paper and bake for 25–30 minutes until golden brown.

5 Cool completely before using your hands to break the crackers into bite-size chunks.

1 cup (105 g) rolled oats
½ cup (50 g) psyllium husks
½ cup (75 g) whole flaxseeds
½ cup (75 g) sunflower seeds
¼ cup (40 g) chia seeds
¼ cup (40 g) black sesame seeds
1 teaspoon sea salt flakes
3 tablespoons coconut oil

Pair with hummus (see page 86) and veggie sticks, olives, and some milk-poached chicken (see page 50) for an epic meze plate.

Make

Want to get creative? Divide the dough into three bowls and add different dried herbs and spices before rolling.

Save

Lasts one week in an airtight container at room temperature.

Tip

If you don't have a rolling pin, use the roll of parchment paper with a couple of rubber bands around it to keep it from unraveling.

Zucchini Fritters

Portions 4 | **Hands-on prep time** 10 minutes

This is a clever way to get everyone to eat more veggies. It's a super-versatile recipe, too: serve these as a side dish or stack them high for a filling weekend breakfast.

2 zucchini, grated or spiralized
2 large eggs, lightly beaten
⅓ cup (40 g) coconut flour
2 scallions, sliced
¼ cup chopped fresh herbs

½ teaspoon sea salt
¼ teaspoon freshly ground
   black pepper
2 tablespoons coconut oil,
   for frying

1 Put the zucchini in a bowl with the eggs, coconut flour, scallions, herbs, salt, and pepper. Mix well until combined. If the mixture is too wet to shape, add a little more flour. If the mixture is too dry, add a little more egg.

2 Heat the coconut oil in a large frying pan over medium-high heat. When the oil is hot, add 2 tablespoons of mixture to the pan and repeat with remaining mixture. Fill the base of the pan but don't let the individual fritters stick together.

3 Fry for about 3 minutes on each side until golden brown. Remove fritters from the pan and drain on paper towel.

I love adding extra flavor with chopped cilantro

Save

Store fritters on a layer of paper towels in an airtight container in the fridge for up to four days, or freeze for up to one month. The paper towels will help keep them crispy.

Tip

If you prefer, replace the coconut flour with almond meal or buckwheat flour.

Whole Roasted Pumpkin

Portions 10 | **Hands-on prep time** 10 minutes

Pumpkin is one of my favorite ingredients. It's sweet, smoky, packed with nutrients, and super versatile in both savory and sweet dishes. Leaving the skin on intensifies the flavor—plus there's minimum effort.

1 Preheat the oven to 400°F.

2 Drizzle the olive oil over the pumpkin, then rub all over to coat.

3 Wrap the pumpkin in parchment paper and then foil. Set it directly on the middle shelf of the oven and bake for 2–2½ hours until tender.

4 Unwrap and roast for another 30 minutes until the skin is dark.

5 Remove the pumpkin from the oven and set it aside to cool completely.

6 Cut the pumpkin into wedges or scoop out the soft flesh

4½ lb (2 kg) whole Japanese pumpkin
3 tablespoons olive oil

Easy eating options

* Stir mashed pumpkin into oats with cinnamon and a drizzle of maple syrup for a delicious breakfast.
* Mash with miso paste and serve with salmon and steamed greens for a quick dinner.
* Use in muffin recipes to replace some of the flour and keep the muffins deliciously moist.
* Cut a small wedge and serve with plain yogurt, chopped pecans, chopped dates, and sea salt for an afternoon snack.
* Add heated coconut milk or water, soy sauce or tamari, and peanut butter, then blend for a deliciously simple Asian-style pumpkin soup.

Save

Store cooked pumpkin flesh in an airtight container in the fridge for up to one week. Freeze portions in ice trays for up to six months and pop out frozen cubes when needed.

Peeling scooping and cubing your
pumpkin before cooking?
I'm over it!

The Perfect Roast Veggies

Portions 6–8 | **Hands-on prep time** 15 minutes

Meal prep is all about speed. Roasted veggies can take forever in the oven, but it's possible to speed up the process. If you're in a serious hurry, opt for veggies grown ABOVE ground for faster roasting times.

1 Preheat the oven to 400°F. Use silicone mats or foil to line three baking sheets.

2 Sort vegetables into similar types on each tray, so that they finish roasting at the same time—that way, you can remove each sheet when it's ready. Pair root vegetables such as sweet potatoes, parsnips, turnips, and carrots together. Brussels sprouts, broccoli, and cauliflower go together; and softer veggies such as zucchini, onions, eggplant, leeks, and peppers go on the final tray.

3 Cut all your veggies so they're about the same size. The smaller the pieces, the faster they roast.

4 Spread the veggies on the trays in one layer. Don't overlap or stack them; they should all have contact with the baking sheet.

5 Drizzle each tray with one-third of the olive oil (3 tablespoons). The oil helps to transfer heat and adds good fat that allows our bodies make the most of the fat-soluble vitamins in the veggies.

6 Sprinkle evenly with the sea salt and roast, removing trays as the veggies are cooked. Cool completely before storing in the fridge.

Seasonal veggies, scrubbed
  but not peeled
¾ cup (185 ml) olive oil
1½ tablespoons sea salt

Toss roasted veggies into the food processor with the Hummus recipe (see page 86)

Make

To reheat veggies, put them in a saucepan with a squeeze of lemon juice to keep them from sticking to the base. Stir regularly for five minutes until warmed through. Alternatively, enjoy them cold with salad (my favorite), or with poached eggs on top.

Save

Store in containers in the fridge for three to four days. You can separate the different veggies or just toss them all into one large container.

Tip

Want to halve the roasting time? Steam the veggies until tender before roasting.

Sticky and Sugarless Caramelized Onions

Portions 10–12 | **Hands-on prep time** 15 minutes

These make a great base for so many dishes. They can be reheated or enjoyed cold. Throw them on top of turkey rissoles or fish cakes, add them to curries, toast, soup, and more.

8 white or red onions, peeled
2 tablespoons olive oil

1 teaspoon sea salt flakes

1   Start by halving each onion through the root. Using a sharp knife, cut a V-shape around the root to remove it. Place the onion flat-side down on a chopping board and slice thinly from one side to the other, or use a mandolin.

2   Heat the olive oil in a wide-based pan (so the onion has room to caramelize, not steam). Add half the onion and cook, stirring, for 1–2 minutes until soft and turning translucent. Add the remaining onion and season with sea salt.

3   Reduce the heat to medium-low and stir occasionally for 15–20 minutes until the onion is very soft. If it starts to stick to the pan, add a splash of hot water and stir.

4   Cool in the pan and then transfer to an airtight container.

Save
Store in an airtight container in the fridge for up to seven days.

Tip
Use bent fingers to hold the bulk of the onion in place. Your knuckles will act as a knife guard.

Sweet and Savory Gluten-Free Pie Crusts

Makes 9-inch pie crust | **Hands-on prep time** 20 minutes

This recipe is also dairy-free and vegan, so you can feed it to everyone! Double the mix and freeze half the dough, or cook the spare crust and freeze it to fill later.

1 Preheat the oven to 400°F. Grease a 9-inch round pie pan with olive oil or coconut oil spray and set aside.

2 In a large bowl, combine all the basic crust ingredients and mix, kneading with your hands when a dough ball forms. If necessary, add a little almond milk (if your dough is a bit dry) or flour (if it's sticky); use your judgment here.

3 Roll out the dough into an 11- to 12-inch circle on a flat surface. I like to roll mine between two sheets of parchment paper, but you can dust your rolling pin and work surface with flour for a similar nonstick situation.

4 Transfer the crust to the pie pan and gently press to fit.

5 Cut away any excess dough with scissors or a knife and bake the crust for 15 minutes.

6 Fill as desired: for a sweet option, try Canadian Pumpkin Pie (see page 110), or for savory, the Apple + Goat Cheese + Sage Quiche (see page 108).

Basic crust

1¼ cups (165 g) buckwheat flour, plus extra for dusting and rolling

1¼ cups (125 g) almond meal

½ teaspoon sea salt flakes

⅛ teaspoon baking powder

½ cup (125 ml) unsweetened almond milk

¼ cup (60 ml) avocado oil or coconut oil (melted)

Sweet crust

+ 1 tablespoon maple syrup

Savory crust

+ 1 tablespoon dried herbs or nutritional yeast

for extra yum

Save

Freeze baked crusts covered in plastic wrap for up to one month, or freeze dough for up to three months.

Apple + Goat Cheese + Sage Quiche

Serves 8 | **Hands-on prep time** 20 minutes

A good quiche is the mainstay of many café menus. I grew up on the stuff. Instead of boring bacon and cheddar, try it with this delicious flavor combo.

1 Preheat the oven to 350°F.

2 Mix the eggs, milk, and rosemary in a bowl.

3 Pour the egg mixture into the precooked pie crust and drop teaspoons of the cheese over the top.

4 Finally, lay the apple slices on top and bake for 35–45 minutes until set.

5 Cool for 5 minutes before removing from the dish and slicing. Garnish with extra rosemary to serve.

12 eggs
¼ cup (60 ml) milk of your choice
1 tablespoon fresh rosemary leaves, plus extra sprigs to serve
1 cooked Savory Gluten-Free Pie Crust (see page 106)
3 oz (80 g) goat cheese or feta cheese
1 small green apple, thinly sliced

Save
Store in the fridge for three to four days. Egg dishes can't be frozen, so make this dish with friends in mind.

Tip
If you have time, sauté some leeks and add them to the egg mixture.

Canadian Pumpkin Pie

Serves 8 | **Hands-on prep time** 15 minutes

I went to Canada recently, and was told SO much about their pumpkin pie. I headed into a famous restaurant where they were serving said pie, with whipped cream. Not one to miss out, I ordered a piece to share with a travel buddy. While it was delicious, it was all kinds of unhealthy, with condensed milk and white sugar. Not the kind of thing I want to be noshing on regularly. This is a simple, healthier take on that mouthwatering pie.

1 Preheat the oven to 350°F.

2 Mix together the pumpkin, eggs, maple syrup, coconut milk, vanilla, salt, and spices. Pour into the precooked pie crust.

3 Bake for 1 hour or until a knife inserted 2 inches from the edge comes out clean (the center of the pie will not be set). Meanwhile, mix together the ingredients for the vanilla maple yogurt.

4 Cool the pie before removing from the pan. Serve with a dollop of vanilla maple yogurt, scattered with star anise, cinnamon, salt, and nutmeg.

2 cups cooked mashed pumpkin (see page 100) or 1 can (15 oz) mashed pumpkin

3 large eggs

½ cup (125 ml) maple syrup, honey, or granulated stevia

½ can (¾ cup + 2 tablespoons) full-fat coconut milk

½ teaspoon vanilla extract

¼ teaspoon sea salt

½ teaspoon ground nutmeg

½ teaspoon ground allspice

2 teaspoons ground cinnamon

1 cooked Sweet Gluten-Free Pie Crust (see page 106)

star anise, cinnamon sticks, salt, and freshly grated nutmeg, to serve

Vanilla maple yogurt

1 cup (260 g) coconut yogurt or plain Greek yogurt

1 teaspoon vanilla bean paste

Save
Store the pie in the fridge for up to four days or freeze for up to one month. Mix up the yogurt ingredients just before eating.

Cauliflower Pizza Crusts

Save half and enjoy it cold for a quick breakfast

Serves 2 | **Hands-on prep time** 10 minutes | **One pizza** = 2 portions

These recipes are for one pizza crust, but I highly recommend doubling or tripling the quantities listed and sticking the extra crusts in the freezer for a super-fast dinner.

1 Preheat the oven to 350°F. Line a baking sheet with a silicone mat or parchment paper.

2 If you're making the vegan version, make a "flax egg" by soaking the flaxseed meal in 2½ tablespoons of water for 5 minutes.

3 Meanwhile, turn the cauliflower into "rice" by grating it (a kitchen grater is fine and easy to clean, but a food processor does an excellent job, too). You should have about 3 cups of rice.

4 Soften the cauliflower in a frying pan over medium heat for 8–10 minutes, stirring with a splash of water so it doesn't stick. (This is optional, but it makes your crust extra crispy by allowing you to squeeze more water out.)

5 Throw the cauliflower into a clean tea towel or muslin cloth and squeeze it to drain as much water as humanly possible. Annoying, but you can count it toward your workout.

6 Put the cauliflower into a bowl with the remaining ingredients (including the "flax egg" if you're making the vegan version) and mix until fully combined.

7 Press the mix into a rectangle on the lined baking sheet. Cook for 30–40 minutes until golden brown.

8 Top with your favorite pizza toppings and bake for another 10 minutes, or allow the untopped crust to cool and then freeze it.

Vegan
1 tablespoon flaxseed meal (to make a "flax egg")
1 large head cauliflower
¼ cup (30 g) chickpea flour
1 teaspoon dried oregano
½ teaspoon sea salt

Nonvegan
1 large head cauliflower
2 tablespoons grated parmesan cheese
1 teaspoon dried oregano
½ teaspoon sea salt
Option: omit the cheese and add an egg

Save

If you plan on freezing a few crusts at a time, put parchment paper between them to prevent them from sticking together. Freeze for up to two months. When you're hungry, just whip out a frozen crust, bake for 10 minutes, then top with your faves and bake again for another 10 minutes.

Tip

It's much easier to make (and store) rectangular pizza crusts.

Leftover Vegetable Bake

Portions 6 | **Hands-on prep time** 10 minutes

When you get to the end of the week and your salad bar is looking a bit sad and sorry, dice up what's left and throw into a baking dish along with any limp-looking herbs. The majority of food waste is unnecessary, and it costs us all a lot of hard-hard-earned cash.

1 Preheat the oven to 350°F.

2 Slice or chop the veggies and toss them together in a baking dish.

3 Mix together the eggs, herbs, milk, and any flavor bombs you like (see pages 20–23) and pour it over the vegetables.

4 Top with parmesan (if using) and bake for 30–40 minutes until set in the middle.

5 Cool for 10 minutes before devouring.

2 cups leftover cooked veggies
12 eggs
½ cup leftover fresh herbs, chopped
½ cup (125 ml) milk of your choice
¼ cup (25 g) finely grated parmesan cheese (optional)

Save
Keep in the fridge for two to three days.

Tip
Make this into portable snacks by using a silicone muffin pan instead and reducing the baking time.

Marinated Chickpeas

Portions 2 | **Hands-on prep time** 5 minutes

This high-protein bowl of goodness is so easy to prepare, and it's delicious as a snack or a side dish.

1   Put the chickpeas into a bowl, along with the onion.

2   Add the cumin, coriander, olive oil, salt, and vinegar. Mix well.

3   Cover and refrigerate.

14 oz (400 g) can chickpeas, rinsed and drained
1 small red onion, thinly sliced
1 teaspoon cumin seeds
1 teaspoon coriander seeds
1 tablespoon olive oil
½ teaspoon sea salt
2 tablespoons red wine vinegar
Fresh thyme leaves, to serve

Make

Save the liquid from the can (it's called aquafaba). It can be whisked into peaks like egg whites. Try using it in the Nut Clusters recipe (see page 138) for a vegan egg white replacement.

Save

Keep for up to five days in the fridge, or freeze for up to one month.

Tip

Make the recipe with canned lentils instead of chickpeas. Prepare both at the same time to keep your options open at each meal.

Anchovy + Broccoli + Pear Soup

Portions 4 | **Hands-on prep time** 25 minutes

This is an awesome way to get acquainted with broccoli: a nice balance of salty anchovies and sweet pear helps to elevate broccoli to another level in this soup!

1 Heat a large saucepan or stockpot over medium heat and add the olive oil, onion, and garlic. Sauté for 5 minutes until softened but not colored. If using Caramelized Onions, you're just warming these through.

2 Chop broccoli into small florets and thinly slice the stems. Add to the pan along with the pear.

3 Pour in the stock or water and bring to a fast simmer, then drop the heat down and gently bubble for 15 minutes or until the broccoli and pear are soft.

4 Add the anchovies and white pepper and blitz with a stick blender until smooth.

5 Remove from the heat and pour in the coconut milk, then stir until well combined.

6 Keep warm and drizzle with coconut milk. Serve sprinkled with herbs, walnuts, and chia seeds, plus a slice of Paleo Bread (see page 90).

2 tablespoons olive oil
2 white onions, chopped (or ½ cup Caramelized Onions— see page 104)
2 garlic cloves, finely sliced
2 medium heads broccoli, including stems (about 1 lb or 500 g)
2 pears, cored and coarsely chopped
4 cups (1 liter) stock or water
12 anchovies
½ teaspoon ground white pepper
1 cup (250 ml) canned coconut milk, plus extra to drizzle
Fresh herbs, chopped walnuts, and chia seeds, to serve

Save

Keep in the fridge for four to five days. Freeze for up to two months.

DIY Vinaigrettes

Hands-on prep time 5 minutes

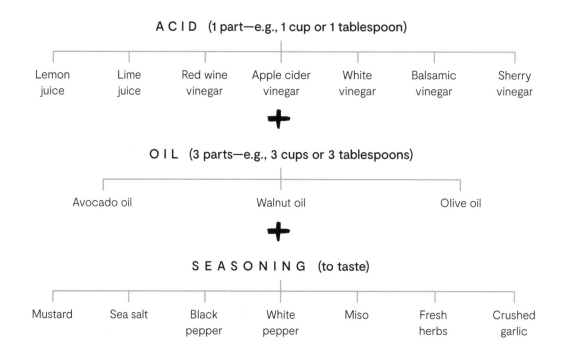

ACID (1 part—e.g., 1 cup or 1 tablespoon)

| Lemon juice | Lime juice | Red wine vinegar | Apple cider vinegar | White vinegar | Balsamic vinegar | Sherry vinegar |

+

OIL (3 parts—e.g., 3 cups or 3 tablespoons)

| Avocado oil | Walnut oil | Olive oil |

+

SEASONING (to taste)

| Mustard | Sea salt | Black pepper | White pepper | Miso | Fresh herbs | Crushed garlic |

Mix

Make a large batch of vinaigrette (say, 1 cup of vinegar and 3 cups of oil) in a glass jar; secure the lid and shake. Want an individual portion? Follow the same formula using tablespoons instead of cups, and whisk with a fork in a small bowl.

Taste

Taste and adjust the flavor to your personal preferences. Need more salt? Lemon? Best to do this by dipping in a salad leaf or veggie stick rather than going in neat.

Store

If you've used only oil, vinegar, salt, and pepper, you can store this in the cupboard in a glass jar for two to three weeks. If you've used fresh ingredients (from the fridge) such as lemon or herbs, store in the fridge for up to five days.

My favorite: apple cider vinegar + olive oil + wholegrain mustard

ALL the Dressings

Makes about 1 cup (250 ml) | **Hands-on prep time** 5–10 minutes

The right dressing can really make or break a dish. I use dressing on nearly everything I eat: roast veggies, eggs, chicken, steamed greens, you name it.

1   Blend or stir all the ingredients together and store in an airtight container in the fridge for up to one week. I use clean recycled glass jars so I can shake them easily.

Pea + almond pesto

1 cup fresh or defrosted frozen peas +
1 cup almonds + 2 garlic cloves + ½ bunch
fresh mint, leaves picked + 1 bunch fresh
basil, leaves picked + ½ cup (125 ml) extra
virgin olive oil + salt + pepper to taste

The simple one

1 cup (260 g) plain
yogurt + 3 tablespoons
dijon mustard
+ 2 teaspoons sriracha

Pea + almond pesto

The simple one

Lemon + tahini

Lemon + tahini

½ cup (135 g) tahini + ½ cup (125 ml) warm water
+ 3 tablespoons lemon juice
+ 1 teaspoon sea salt + 2 garlic cloves, crushed

Miso + almond

½ cup (140 g) almond butter + ⅓ cup (80 ml) warm water + 2 tablespoons apple cider vinegar + 1 tablespoon miso paste + 1 tablespoon sesame oil
+ 1 tablespoon raw honey or maple syrup (optional)
+ 2 garlic cloves, crushed

Coconut tzatziki

1 cup (260 g) coconut yogurt + ¼ cup finely chopped cucumber + 3 tablespoons lemon juice
+ 1 tablespoon chopped dill + ½ teaspoon sea salt

The green one

4 tablespoons lime juice + 4 tablespoons tahini + 3 tablespoons extra virgin olive oil + 2 tablespoons mustard + 1 bunch fresh cilantro, leaves picked + 1 teaspoon ground ginger + 1 teaspoon ground coriander + 1 tablespoon honey or 10 drops liquid stevia + salt + pepper

Coconut tzatziki

Miso + almond

The green one

Quick Pickles

Portions 6–8 per jar | **Hands-on prep time** 10 minutes per jar

I love quick pickles (aka refrigerator pickles). They don't produce the deep flavor (or bacterial goodness) of their fermented counterparts, BUT they're ready in a few hours and save you precious time "canning" them. Store them in the refrigerator and throw them onto anything you like: salads, savory oats, fish dishes, goddess bowls—you get the picture.

Did you know? White vinegar shares similar health properties to the revered apple cider version. Both are high in acetic acid, which is said to kill harmful bacteria, stabilize blood sugar, and slow digestion to keep you fuller for longer.

1   Combine the vinegar, mustard seeds, and cumin seeds in a large saucepan. Bring to a boil over medium-high heat.

2   Pack the chopped veggies into clean glass jars, leaving a little space at the top for the vinegar to completely immerse them.

3   Pour the hot liquid over the veggies until the jar is full. Cool the jars to room temperature, then secure the lids and refrigerate.

Save

Pickled veggies can be eaten after a few short hours, but will last up to one month in the fridge.

Rainbow chard

Fennel + fronds + stems

Pickle liquid

For a 1 quart (1 liter) jar
(quantities are approximate)
2 cups (500 ml) white vinegar
½ **teaspoon mustard seeds**
½ **teaspoon cumin seeds**
½ **teaspoon sea salt**

My favorite veggie combos

4 cups sliced, chopped, or julienned vegetables
* celery + cucumber + cauliflower
* carrot + carrot tops + radish
* fennel + fronds + stems
* red onion
* whatever you have on hand

Carrot + carrot tops + radish

Celery + cauliflower

Red onion

Celery

Rainbow chard

DIY Trail Mix

Portions 5 (1 oz or 30 g servings) | **Hands-on prep time** 10 minutes

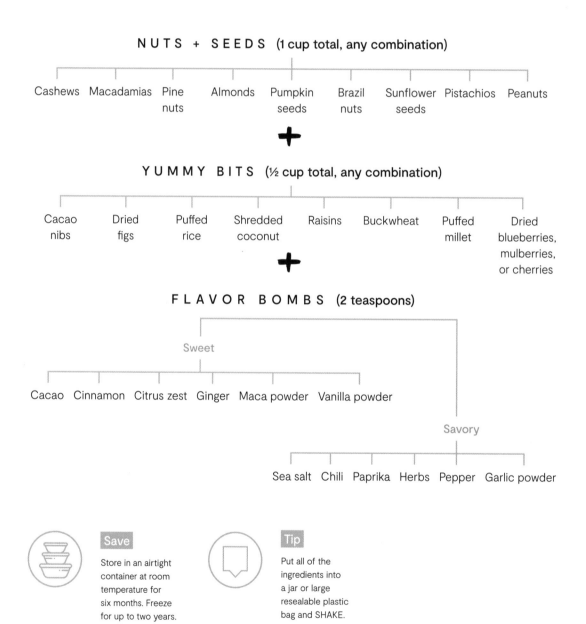

NUTS + SEEDS (1 cup total, any combination)

Cashews   Macadamias   Pine nuts   Almonds   Pumpkin seeds   Brazil nuts   Sunflower seeds   Pistachios   Peanuts

+

YUMMY BITS (½ cup total, any combination)

Cacao nibs   Dried figs   Puffed rice   Shredded coconut   Raisins   Buckwheat   Puffed millet   Dried blueberries, mulberries, or cherries

+

FLAVOR BOMBS (2 teaspoons)

Sweet

Cacao   Cinnamon   Citrus zest   Ginger   Maca powder   Vanilla powder

Savory

Sea salt   Chili   Paprika   Herbs   Pepper   Garlic powder

Save
Store in an airtight container at room temperature for six months. Freeze for up to two years.

Tip
Put all of the ingredients into a jar or large resealable plastic bag and SHAKE.

Cashews + Shredded coconut + Lime zest + Chili flakes

Almonds + Cacao nibs +
Coconut flakes + Cocoa powder

Pine nuts + Macadamias + Chopped dried figs + Finely chopped rosemary
+ Sea salt flakes

Sweet + Savory Freezer Truffles

Portions 10 (2 dates) | **Hands-on prep time** 10 minutes

Ever feel like you just need a little somethin' somethin' to round off a meal, but you're probably not actually hungry? Rather than reaching for the nearest chocolate bar, grab these awesome little mouthfuls from your freezer. Freezing the dates firms them up and makes them deliciously chewy, just like caramels. STUFF THEM WITH YUMMY THINGS in less than a minute and devour. Perfection.

1   Grab a few cups of medjool dates (the big, juicy ones) and pit them all.

2   Chuck them in an airtight container and freeze (for up to two months).

3   When you want a quick snack or after-dinner treat, grab a few and stuff them with some of your favorite fillings. Ideas below.

Savory

* 1 walnut + 1 teaspoon blue cheese
* 1 olive + 1 teaspoon hummus (see page 86)
* Basil leaf + small cube of cheddar cheese

Sweet

* 1 teaspoon almond butter + sea salt
* 1 pecan + 1 square of dark chocolate
* 1 teaspoon coconut butter + ground cinnamon

Salted Chocolate Banana Bread

Portions 12 | **Hands-on prep time** 20 minutes

I'd never tried banana bread until I moved to Australia. It's a blessing in disguise: delicious but often packed with refined flour and sugar. This version, however, is not! I have this toasted for a weekend breakfast and keep slices in the freezer ready to go.

1 Preheat the oven to 350°F. Line a 9 x 5 inch loaf pan with parchment paper or use a silicone loaf pan sprayed with cooking spray.

2 In a large bowl, mix the nut meal, cocoa powder, baking powder, baking soda, salt, and cinnamon. Set aside.

3 In a separate bowl, beat together the eggs, coconut sugar, coconut oil, vanilla, and milk. Fold in the mashed banana.

4 Pour the wet ingredients into the dry ingredients, mixing well.

5 Pour the batter into the loaf pan and sprinkle with the salt flakes.

6 Bake for 55 minutes or until a knife inserted in the center comes out clean.

7 Cool for 20 minutes in the pan before turning out. Cool completely before slicing.

1¼ cups (125 g) almond or hazelnut meal
½ cup (65 g) cocoa powder, sifted
1 teaspoon baking powder
1 teaspoon baking soda
1 teaspoon sea salt
2 teaspoons ground cinnamon
2 large eggs
⅓ cup (50 g) coconut sugar
⅓ cup (80 ml) melted coconut oil
2 teaspoons vanilla extract
1½ tablespoons milk of your choice
4 small bananas, mashed

Topping
1 teaspoon sea salt flakes

Save

Store in an airtight container in the fridge for three to four days. Slice and freeze between pieces of parchment paper for up to six weeks.

Salted Caramel

Makes 1 jar (about 12 portions) | **Hands-on prep time** 5 minutes

Throw this on your overnight oats, on pancakes and waffles, spread it on a banana as a snack, or add a tablespoon to smoothies.

1 Put all of the ingredients except the salt in a food processor and blitz until smooth, or stick it in a bowl and get whisking to make it lump-free.

2 Stir the salt flakes through and transfer to a glass jar.

½ cup (125 ml) maple syrup
½ cup (125 ml) canned coconut milk
½ cup (125 ml) melted coconut oil
⅓ cup (90 g) natural almond butter
1½ teaspoons sea salt flakes

Save

Store at room temperature for up to one week. Freeze leftovers in an ice tray and add to smoothies.

Cardamom + Chocolate + Cherry Tray-Baked Oats

Portions 10 | **Hands-on prep time** 15 minutes

Admittedly, this recipe has a few more ingredients than I'd usually bother with, but I promise it's oh-so-worth it. It doubles as breakfast and dessert.

1 Preheat the oven to 350°F.

2 In a mixing bowl, combine the oats, nuts, cinnamon, cocoa powder, baking powder, salt, and cardamom.

3 Make a well in the center and add the milk, egg, sweetener, butter or oil, and vanilla. Mix these together before incorporating the oat mixture.

4 Add the cherries and chocolate chips (if using) and give it all a good stir.

5 Pour the mix into a deep baking sheet and spread it out with the back of a spoon. Mine is usually about 1 inch (2.5 cm) thick, but if yours is thinner, you can shave off a bit of the bake time.

6 Bake for 45 minutes, then remove and cool for 5 minutes before spooning some into a bowl and devouring.

2 cups (210 g) rolled oats

⅔ cup (85 g) coarsely chopped pecans or almonds

2 teaspoons ground cinnamon

¼ cup (25 g) cocoa powder

1 teaspoon baking powder

½ teaspoon sea salt

1 teaspoon ground cardamom

2 cups (500 ml) milk of your choice

3 large eggs or "flax eggs" (see page 112)

⅓ cup (80 ml) maple syrup, honey, or granulated stevia

3 tablespoons melted butter or coconut oil

2 teaspoons vanilla extract

2½ cups cherries (fresh or frozen)

½ cup (85 g) dark chocolate chips or cacao nibs (optional)

No cherries? Try blackberries, blueberries, or raspberries

Make

Optional toppings for serving: plain yogurt + a drizzle of maple syrup or honey + extra chocolate chips or cacao nibs.

Save

Store in an airtight container in the fridge for up to one week. Freeze as individual portions for up to two months.

Raspberry + Peanut Butter Mud Slice

Portions 12 | **Hands-on prep time** 15 minutes

Kinda like a deliciously moist brownie, this slice pretends to be a decadent treat. Don't let it fool you: it's sugar-free and packed with fiber for healthy digestion.

1 Preheat the oven to 350°F. Line a 13 x 9 inch baking pan with parchment paper or spray with cooking spray.

2 Put the cannellini beans and peanut butter in a food processor and blend until smooth, then add the almond meal, baking powder, eggs, vanilla, stevia, and salt.

3 Fold the raspberries through the batter and pour it into the brownie pan. Scatter ¼ cup of peanuts on top, if using.

4 Bake for 40 minutes until the center is just set.

5 Cool completely before cutting into squares.

15.5 oz can cannellini (or other white) beans, drained and rinsed
½ cup (140 g) peanut butter
1 cup (100 g) almond meal
1 teaspoon baking powder
3 large eggs or "flax eggs" (see page 112)
2 teaspoons vanilla extract
⅔ cup (120 g) granulated stevia
½ teaspoon sea salt
5 oz raspberries (frozen or fresh)
peanuts, to scatter (optional)

Save

Store in an airtight container in the fridge for up to five days. Freeze for up to two months.

Nut Clusters

Makes 30 | **Hands-on prep time** 10 minutes

Packed with fiber, vitamins, and antioxidants, nuts are in my diet every day. Portion control is important with these clusters: try not to eat half the batch in one sitting!

1 Preheat the oven to 350°F. Line two large baking sheets with parchment paper.

2 In a bowl, whisk the egg whites until frothy, then fold in the nuts, fruit, cinnamon, and salt, until well coated.

3 Spoon large dollops of mixture onto the baking sheets and bake for 10 minutes or until golden. Cool on the trays.

3 egg whites
1¼ lb (600 g) unsalted mixed nuts
5 oz (150 g) dried fruit, such as
figs and raisins, chopped
1-2 teaspoons ground cinnamon
1 teaspoon sea salt (optional)

I love cashews, almonds, pistachios, and pine nuts

 Save
Store in the fridge for up to one week. Keep them in the freezer for up to one month, for the best portion control!

 Tip
Make chocolatey versions by adding 2 teaspoons of cocoa powder instead of the cinnamon.

Blender Cookie Dough

Portions 10 | **Hands-on prep time** 10 minutes

This is my favorite Friday-night treat. Arguably healthier than a tub of a certain cookie dough ice cream that I used to indulge in way too often. Zero guilt allowed.

1 Put the oats, cashews, and almond meal into a food processor and blend to the consistency of flour.

2 Add melted coconut oil and honey or maple syrup and process again.

3 Remove from the food processor and stir in the chocolate chips or cacao nibs.

4 Store in an airtight container in the fridge for up to two weeks, so you'll be ready when sweet cravings hit.

¾ cup (75 g) rolled oats
¾ cup (120 g) cashews
   (or more oats)
1½ cups (150 g) almond meal
3 tablespoons coconut oil
4 tablespoons honey or
   maple syrup
½ cup (85 g) chocolate chips
   or cacao nibs

Save

These are freezer-friendly, so if you struggle with portion control like me, roll into balls or press into cubes and freeze for up to three months.

Fruit Crumble Duo

Portions 6 | **Hands-on prep time** 20 minutes

Oh crumble! Our love affair has been long and wonderful. When I can't decide which filling I want, I make two in one pan. That's genius right there.

1 Preheat the oven to 350°F.

For the crumble

2 In a large bowl, mix the oats, almond meal, cinnamon, and salt.

3 Next, add the coconut oil or butter and rub the mixture together between your fingers until a crumbly texture forms.

4 Add the sweetener (if using) and stir with a wooden spoon.

For the fruit

5 Set two small saucepans over medium heat. Put the blackberries in one and the apple in the other, along with ½ cup (125 ml) of water (hot from the kettle to speed things up) in each saucepan.

6 Stir half the stevia and half the lemon juice into each pan.

7 Gently simmer, uncovered, for 8–10 minutes until the fruit is soft and the liquid has reduced by half.

8 Spoon the blackberries into one side of a baking dish, and spoon the apple into the other side. Don't worry if the juices mix together; it will all taste delicious.

9 Add the crumble topping and bake for 30 minutes or until the topping is golden brown.

Crumble

1½ cups (160 g) rolled oats
1 cup (100 g) almond meal
2 teaspoons ground cinnamon
1 teaspoon sea salt
3 tablespoons coconut oil (solid)
  or butter
3 tablespoons rice malt syrup
  or sweetener of your choice
  (optional)

Filling

3 cups blackberries (fresh
  or frozen)
3 cups chopped apple
1 lemon
½ cup granulated stevia or
  other sweetener

Add the lemon zest, too, for extra zing

Save

Store in the fridge for five days; freeze for up to two months.

Tip

If you live in a warm country like Australia, pop coconut oil in the fridge for a couple of hours to keep it solid.

Two-Ingredient Sweet Treats

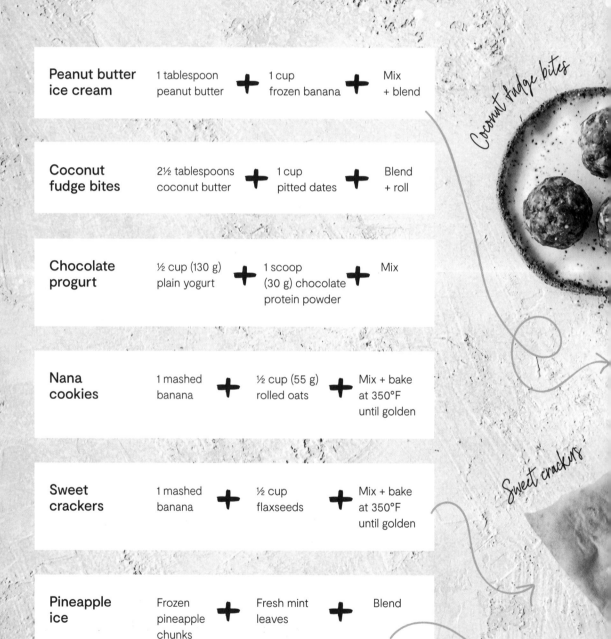

Peanut butter ice cream   1 tablespoon peanut butter **+** 1 cup frozen banana **+** Mix + blend

Coconut fudge bites   2½ tablespoons coconut butter **+** 1 cup pitted dates **+** Blend + roll

Chocolate progurt   ½ cup (130 g) plain yogurt **+** 1 scoop (30 g) chocolate protein powder **+** Mix

Nana cookies   1 mashed banana **+** ½ cup (55 g) rolled oats **+** Mix + bake at 350°F until golden

Sweet crackers   1 mashed banana **+** ½ cup flaxseeds **+** Mix + bake at 350°F until golden

Pineapple ice   Frozen pineapple chunks **+** Fresh mint leaves **+** Blend

Coconut fudge bites

Sweet crackers

Chocolate progurt

Peanut butter ice cream

Nana cookies

Pineapple ice

DIY Bliss Balls

Makes 15 | **Hands-on prep time** 10 minutes

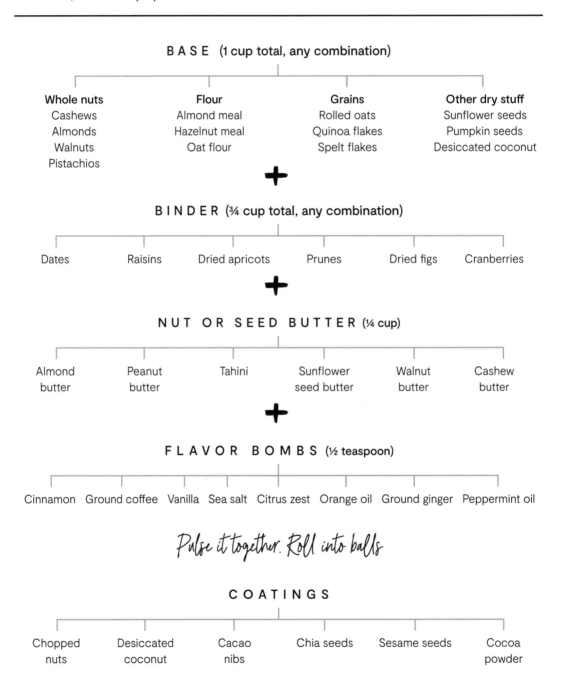

B A S E (1 cup total, any combination)

Whole nuts	Flour	Grains	Other dry stuff
Cashews	Almond meal	Rolled oats	Sunflower seeds
Almonds	Hazelnut meal	Quinoa flakes	Pumpkin seeds
Walnuts	Oat flour	Spelt flakes	Desiccated coconut
Pistachios			

+

B I N D E R (¾ cup total, any combination)

Dates   Raisins   Dried apricots   Prunes   Dried figs   Cranberries

+

N U T   O R   S E E D   B U T T E R (¼ cup)

Almond butter   Peanut butter   Tahini   Sunflower seed butter   Walnut butter   Cashew butter

+

F L A V O R   B O M B S (½ teaspoon)

Cinnamon   Ground coffee   Vanilla   Sea salt   Citrus zest   Orange oil   Ground ginger   Peppermint oil

Pulse it together. Roll into balls

C O A T I N G S

Chopped nuts   Desiccated coconut   Cacao nibs   Chia seeds   Sesame seeds   Cocoa powder

Four-Ingredient Chocolate-Chip Cookies

Makes 15 | **Hands-on prep time** 15 minutes

You can't have a meal-prep plan without cookies: where's the balance in that? Keep it simple and nutritious with these four ingredients.

1 Preheat the oven to 350°F. Line a baking sheet with parchment paper.

2 Put the tahini and maple syrup into a saucepan over low heat.

3 Mix until well combined, remove from heat, and stir in the almond meal and cacao nibs or chocolate chips.

4 Scoop out a heaping tablespoon of dough and roll it into a ball between your hands, then place on the prepared baking sheet and press down with your hands to flatten. Sprinkle with salt, if using.

5 Bake for 10–12 minutes and cool before transferring to an airtight container.

1 cup (270 g) tahini
⅓ cup (80 ml) maple syrup
2 cups (200 g) almond meal
3 tablespoons cacao nibs or dark chocolate chips
½ teaspoon sea salt (optional)

Save

Store in the fridge for up to seven days, or freeze for up to one month.

Step 3

PUT IT
TOGETHER

Poached Egg Combos

I love eggs for breakfast, lunch, and dinner! Keep them interesting with these combos. Combo 1 adds scallions and chili to yogurt for a surprisingly zingy flavor fest.

COMBO 1

| Poached Egg | Paleo Bread | Yogurt | Parsley |
| Page 45 | Page 90 | | |

PLUS scallions, chili flakes, sesame seeds, paprika

COMBO 2

| Poached Egg | Salmon Gravlax | Avocado | Lemon juice |
| Page 45 | Page 40 | | |

COMBO 3

| Poached Egg | Spicy Ground Bison | Salad greens | Brown rice |
| Page 45 | Page 70 | | Page 89 |

Salmon Gravlax Combos

Gravlax is the ultimate easy-to-make luxury food. Use sushi-grade salmon for the best results. Pair it with sharp flavors and contrasting textures for a memorable meal or snack.

COMBO 1

| Salmon Gravlax | Zucchini Fritters | Coconut tzatziki dressing Page 123 | Pepper |
| Page 40 | Page 98 | | |

PLUS lemon zest, dill

COMBO 2

| Salmon Gravlax | Oaty Seed Crackers | Goat cheese | Pepper |
| Page 40 | Page 96 | | |

COMBO 3

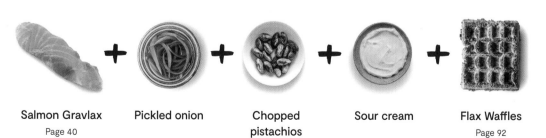

| Salmon Gravlax | Pickled onion | Chopped pistachios | Sour cream | Flax Waffles |
| Page 40 | | | | Page 92 |

Falafel Combos

This Middle Eastern fave is a dish even nonvegetarians love. Perfect served simply with hummus or a tangy dressing, falafel is even better with these combos.

COMBO 1

| Nut Butter Falafel | Hummus | Corn tortilla | Pea + almond pesto |
| Page 54 | Page 86 | | Page 122 |

PLUS red onion, cucumber, herbs

COMBO 2

| Nut Butter Falafel | Marinated Chickpeas Page 116 | Salad greens | Coconut tzatziki dressing Page 123 | Dried apricots, chopped |
| Page 54 | | | | |

COMBO 3

| Nut Butter Falafel | Perfect Roast Veggies | Black Bean Hummus | Olive oil |
| Page 54 | Page 102 | Page 86 | |

Smoky Turkey Rissole Combos

Turkey meat helps support healthy levels of serotonin in the body, which makes it good-mood food.
Try making ground turkey into burgers, meatballs, or rissoles and eating them in a salad,
with veggies, or—my favorite—on Flax Waffles.

COMBO 1

Smoky Turkey Rissoles Page 66	Flax Waffles Page 92	Pea + almond pesto Page 122	Salad greens

PLUS   tomatoes, dried chili flakes, black pepper, herbs

COMBO 2

Smoky Turkey Rissoles Page 66	Spiralized veggies	The green one dressing Page 123	Tomatoes

COMBO 3

Smoky Turkey Rissoles Page 66	Perfect Roast Veggies Page 102	Quinoa Page 89	Avocado	Cilantro

Healthy Fish Cake Combos

These fish cakes are a hero in your fridge. Pair with a crisp salad and a squeeze of lemon, plus other prepped goodies—the combos are limited only by your imagination.

COMBO 1

Healthy Fish Cakes
Pages 62–63

Pickles

White Bean Hummus
Page 86

Salad greens

PLUS capers, lemon, parsley, scallions, yogurt dressing, pepper

COMBO 2

Healthy Fish Cakes Pages 62–63

Corn tortilla

Avocado

Salad greens

The simple one dressing Page 122

COMBO 3

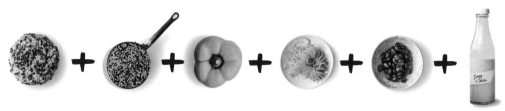

Healthy Fish Cakes Pages 62–63

Quinoa Page 89

Diced pepper

Spiralized carrot

Pomegranate seeds

Lemon + tahini dressing Page 123

Satay Tofu Crumble Combos

Packed with calcium, tofu is an awesome source of your daily dose of that nutrient.
Pair with veggies, nuts, and herbs for a fast and delicious meal.

COMBO 1

| **Satay Tofu Crumble** | **Perfect Roast Veggies** | **Brown rice** | **Peanuts** |
| Page 64 | Page 102 | Page 89 | |

PLUS herbs

COMBO 2

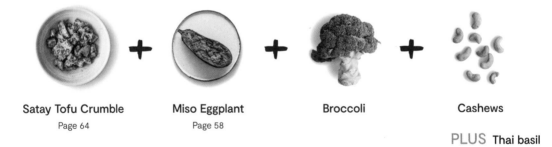

| **Satay Tofu Crumble** | **Miso Eggplant** | **Broccoli** | **Cashews** |
| Page 64 | Page 58 | | |

PLUS Thai basil

COMBO 3

| **Satay Tofu Crumble** | **Roasted Pumpkin Mash** | **Miso** | **Miso + almond dressing** | **Cauliflower Steaks** Page 56 | **Chopped almonds** |
| Page 64 | Page 100 | | Page 123 | | |

Cauliflower Steak Combos

These steaks make a great base for your favorite protein. Pile it up on top and add the dressing of your choice from pages 122–23.

COMBO 1

Cauliflower Steaks
Page 56

+

Pea + almond pesto
Page 122

+

Poached Egg
Page 45

+

Black pepper

PLUS herbs, salt, chili oil

COMBO 2

Cauliflower Steaks Page 56

+

Pea + almond pesto Page 122

+

Tomatoes

+

Pine nuts

+

Milk-Poached Chicken Page 50

COMBO 3

Cauliflower Steaks Page 56

+

Lemon-Broiled Striped Bass Page 60

+

Salad greens

+

Lentil Hummus
Page 86

+

Marinated Chickpeas Page 116

Zucchini Fritter Combos

Eat zucchini fritters hot or cold. Use them as the base of a meal or crumble them on top of veggies, grains, or salad greens. Add a tangy dressing for a contrast of flavor.

COMBO 1

Zucchini Fritters	Marinated Chickpeas	The green one	Julienned cucumber
Page 98	Page 116	dressing Page 123	

PLUS pecans, pickled celery, fennel, carrot, onion, lemon wedges, cilantro

COMBO 2

Zucchini Fritters	Lemon-Broiled	Cilantro	Teff	Vinaigrette
Page 98	Striped Bass Page 60		Page 89	Page 120

COMBO 3

Zucchini Fritters	Feta	Roasted Pumpkin	Pepper	Olive oil
Page 98		Mash Page 100		

The green one

One-Tray Chicken Combos

There are three types of seasoning for oven-baked chicken on pages 48–49, or use your own favorite. Once the chicken is cooked, add sweet or savory accompaniments to keep it interesting for every meal. Some of my favorite additions include lime, mango, and herbs.

COMBO 1

One-Tray Chicken: Lemon + Rosemary
Pages 48–49

+

Coconut tzatziki dressing Page 123

+

Pickled celery
Pages 124–25

+

Olive oil

PLUS walnuts, apples, grapes, salad greens, herbs

COMBO 2

One-Tray Chicken: Spicy Barbecue
Pages 48–49

+ Avocado

+ Mango

+ Tomatoes

+ Lime juice

+ Black beans

PLUS chili

COMBO 3

One-Tray Chicken: Maple Sesame
Pages 48–49

+ Brown rice
Page 89

+ Arugula

+ Pea + almond pesto Page 122

+ Tomatoes

+ Basil

PLUS almonds

Hummus Combos

You might say that I'm obsessed with hummus. How do I eat you?
Let me count the ways . . .

COMBO 1

White Bean Hummus
Page 86

+

Nut Butter Falafel
Page 54

+

Radish

+

Vinaigrette
Page 120

PLUS tomatoes, black sesame seeds, salad greens, pomegranate seeds

COMBO 2

Black Bean Hummus Page 86

+

Oaty Seed Crackers
Page 96

+

Satay Tofu Crumble
Page 64

COMBO 3

Lentil Hummus Page 86

+

Paleo Bread
Page 90

+

Canned tuna

+

Sesame seeds

Oven-Baked Salmon Combos

Salmon is rich in omega-3s, which have been shown to reduce inflammation in the gut.
I enjoy this fish a few times a week with fresh herbs, grains, and spices.

COMBO 1

Foolproof
Oven-Baked Salmon
Pages 42–43

+

Quinoa
Page 89

+

Moroccan spice mix

+

Pomegranate seeds

PLUS hazelnuts, raisins, herbs, vinaigrette

COMBO 2

Foolproof Oven-
Baked Salmon
Pages 42–43

+

Mint

+

Peas

+

Arugula

+

Pine nuts

COMBO 3

Foolproof Oven-
Baked Salmon
Pages 42–43

+

Cucumber

+

Avocado

+

Corn

+

Radish

+

Vinaigrette
Page 120

Cooked Shrimp Combos

I always keep cooked shrimp in my freezer. They defrost quickly, and can be eaten cold or quickly heated through. They turn any salad, veggies, or leftovers into a meal in a flash.

COMBO 1

Cooked Shrimp
Page 25

Corn

Avocado

Tomatoes

PLUS chili flakes, fresh chili, mango, black beans, lime, salad greens, herbs

COMBO 2

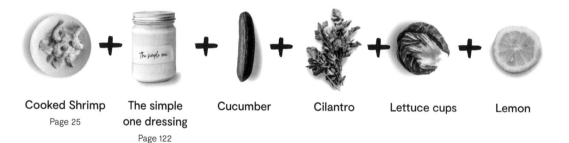

Cooked Shrimp
Page 25

The simple
one dressing
Page 122

Cucumber

Cilantro

Lettuce cups

Lemon

COMBO 3

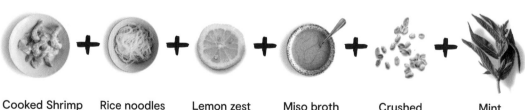

Cooked Shrimp
Page 25

Rice noodles

Lemon zest

Miso broth

Crushed
peanuts

Mint

Asian-Style Ground Turkey Combos

Forget takeout: just a few simple combos with this spicy Asian-style dish will have you assembling restaurant-quality dishes in no time.

COMBO 1

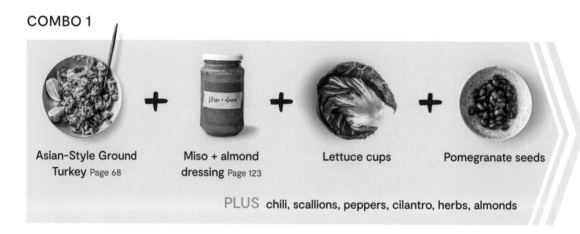

Asian-Style Ground Turkey Page 68　　　+　　　**Miso + almond dressing** Page 123　　　+　　　**Lettuce cups**　　　+　　　**Pomegranate seeds**

PLUS chili, scallions, peppers, cilantro, herbs, almonds

COMBO 2

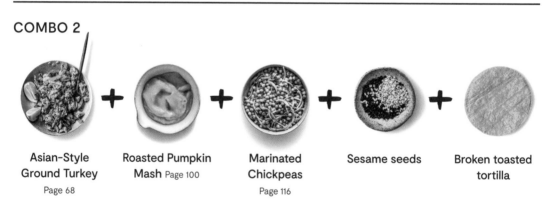

Asian-Style Ground Turkey Page 68　　+　　**Roasted Pumpkin Mash** Page 100　　+　　**Marinated Chickpeas** Page 116　　+　　**Sesame seeds**　　+　　**Broken toasted tortilla**

COMBO 3

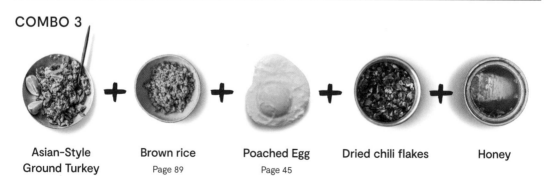

Asian-Style Ground Turkey Page 68　　+　　**Brown rice** Page 89　　+　　**Poached Egg** Page 45　　+　　**Dried chili flakes**　　+　　**Honey**

Spiralized Veggie Combos

Whether you spiralize them yourself or buy them already shredded from the supermarket (remember, shortcuts are totally okay!) these curly veggie strings make a nutritious and fun base for any meal. Steam them, add them to a stir-fry, or eat them raw if you love that crunch.

COMBO 1

Spiralized veggies   +   Lemon + tahini dressing Page 122   +   Marinated Chickpeas Page 116   +   Avocado

PLUS sesame seeds, scallions, parsley

COMBO 2

Spiralized veggies   +   Arugula   +   Parmesan cheese   +   Pine nuts   +   Olive oil

COMBO 3

Spiralized veggies   +   One-Tray Chicken Pages 48–49   +   Cilantro   +   Lemon   +   Cashews

DIY Muesli Combos

I love to start a weekend with a bowl of peanutty chocolate muesli—and when you make your own mixture of muesli as a base, breakfast will never be the same.

COMBO 1

DIY Muesli
Page 78

Cacao nibs

Peanuts

Cinnamon

PLUS buckwheat groats, freeze-dried banana, vanilla powder, toasted coconut

COMBO 2

DIY Muesli
Page 78

Almond milk

Fresh banana slices

Maple syrup

COMBO 3

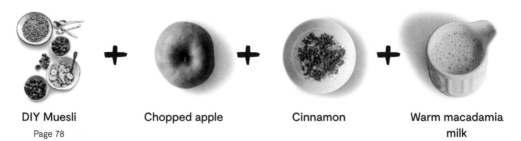

DIY Muesli
Page 78

Chopped apple

Cinnamon

Warm macadamia milk

Blender Cookie Dough Combos

I know you probably just want to spoon this sweet treat straight into your mouth (no judgment), but you can take it to the NEXT LEVEL with these additions.

COMBO 1

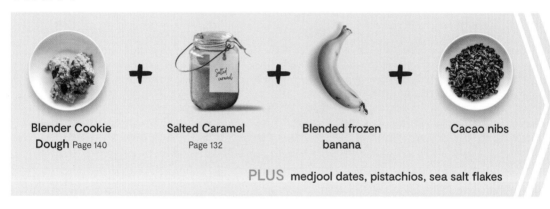

Blender Cookie
Dough Page 140
+
Salted Caramel
Page 132
+
Blended frozen
banana
+
Cacao nibs

PLUS medjool dates, pistachios, sea salt flakes

COMBO 2

Blender Cookie
Dough Page 140
+
Apple slices
+
Raisins
+
Nutmeg

COMBO 3

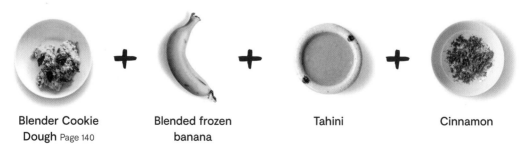

Blender Cookie
Dough Page 140
+
Blended frozen
banana
+
Tahini
+
Cinnamon

Frozen Banana Combos

Not only are bananas loaded with fiber and vitamins, they're the perfect blender buddy for smoothies and creamy desserts. I have tons of them in my freezer year-round. Tip: Peel and slice them before freezing; it's so much easier.

COMBO 1

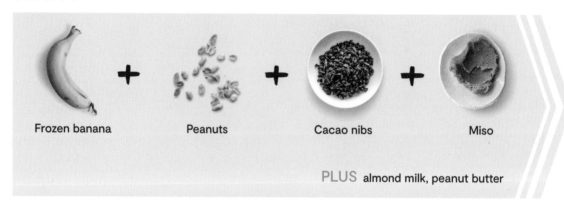

Frozen banana　+　Peanuts　+　Cacao nibs　+　Miso

PLUS almond milk, peanut butter

COMBO 2

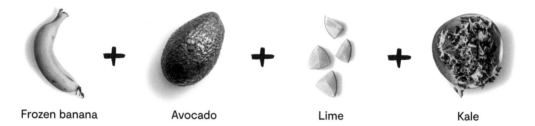

Frozen banana　+　Avocado　+　Lime　+　Kale

PLUS coconut milk

COMBO 3

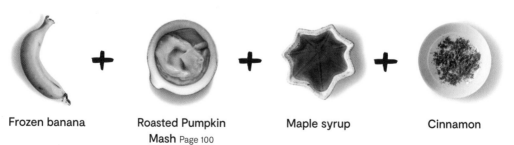

Frozen banana　+　Roasted Pumpkin Mash Page 100　+　Maple syrup　+　Cinnamon

PLUS coconut milk, nutmeg, oats

Supergrain Combos

Packed with fiber, whole grains form the base for dishes that help keep you feeling satisfied, and help control your blood-sugar levels, too.

COMBO 1

Freekeh
Page 89

Sticky and Sugarless Caramelized Onions
Page 104

Roasted Pumpkin Mash with miso
Page 100

Poached Egg
Page 45

PLUS arugula

COMBO 2

Freekeh
Page 89

Brown rice
Page 89

Toasted coconut flakes

Garlic

Ginger

PLUS coconut milk, sea salt

COMBO 3

Freekeh
Page 89

Sticky and Sugarless Caramelized Onions
Page 104

Teff
Page 89

Foolproof Oven-Baked Salmon Pages 42–43

Mint

PLUS feta, parsley, chopped dates

Lemon-Broiled Striped Bass Combos

Striped bass is a white-fleshed fish found along the Atlantic coast of North America. Pair this tasty seafood with healthy fats and fiber for a balanced meal.

COMBO 1

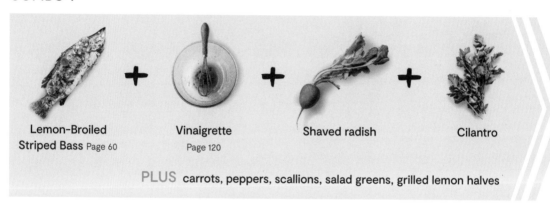

Lemon-Broiled Striped Bass Page 60 **+** Vinaigrette Page 120 **+** Shaved radish **+** Cilantro

PLUS carrots, peppers, scallions, salad greens, grilled lemon halves

COMBO 2

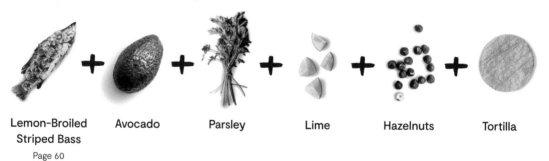

Lemon-Broiled Striped Bass Page 60 **+** Avocado **+** Parsley **+** Lime **+** Hazelnuts **+** Tortilla

COMBO 3

Lemon-Broiled Striped Bass Page 60 **+** Pea + almond pesto Page 122 **+** Perfect Roast Veggies Page 102

Salted Choc Banana Bread Combos

You will be amazed at the flavor combinations that taste great on this rich chocolate dessert loaf.

COMBO 1

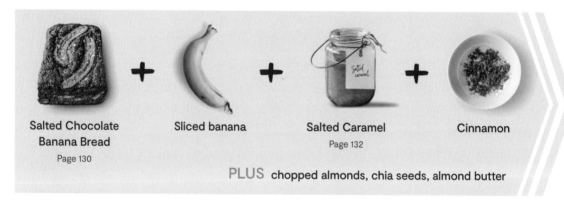

Salted Chocolate Banana Bread
Page 130

Sliced banana

Salted Caramel
Page 132

Cinnamon

PLUS chopped almonds, chia seeds, almond butter

COMBO 2

Salted Chocolate Banana Bread Page 130

Ricotta cheese

Honey

Pistachios

COMBO 3

Salted Chocolate Banana Bread Page 130

Mashed raspberries

Peanut butter

Flax Waffle Combos

Toast up these waffles and top them with savory or sweet flavors for breakfast, lunch, or dessert.

COMBO 1

Flax Waffles	Boiled Eggs	The green one	Pepper
Page 92	Page 44	dressing Page 123	

PLUS avocado, chopped kale, crumbled seed crackers

COMBO 2

Flax Waffles	Milk-Poached Chicken	Lemon + tahini	Arugula
Page 92	Page 50	dressing Page 122	

COMBO 3

Flax Waffles	Cinnamon	Blueberries	Blender Cookie Dough
Page 92			Page 140

Milk-Poached Chicken Combos

Add different sauces, spices, and textures to make this tender chicken even more delicious.

COMBO 1

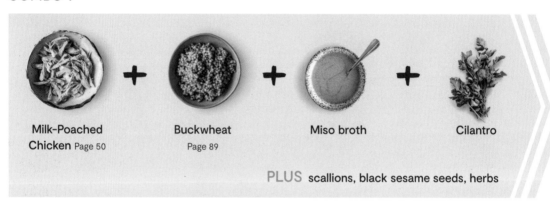

Milk-Poached
Chicken Page 50

Buckwheat
Page 89

Miso broth

Cilantro

PLUS scallions, black sesame seeds, herbs

COMBO 2

Milk-Poached
Chicken Page 50

Cauliflower Steaks
Page 56

Pea + almond pesto
Page 122

Pomegranate seeds

COMBO 3

Milk-Poached
Chicken Page 50

The simple one
dressing Page 122

Salad greens

Chopped
avocado

Toasted coconut
flakes

Roasted Pumpkin Combos

Roasted pumpkin is naturally sweet. I love to pair it with salty flavors for balance.

COMBO 1

Roasted Pumpkin
Page 100

Feta

Honey

Arugula

PLUS pumpkin seeds, spinach, pepper, rosemary

COMBO 2

Roasted Pumpkin
Page 100

Lime

Soy sauce

Peanut butter

blend and heat with enough coconut milk to make a soup

COMBO 3

Roasted Pumpkin
Page 100

**Satay Tofu
Crumble** Page 64

Broccoli

Sesame oil

Scallions

Miso Eggplant Combos

Pair this salty–sweet roasted vegetable with veggies or your favorite protein
to make a simple umami delight.

COMBO 1

Miso Eggplant
Page 58

+

Spiralized veggies

+

Pickled Eggs
Page 47

+

Brown rice
Page 89

PLUS scallions, herbs, pickled ginger, chili, sesame seeds, brown rice, soy sauce, tofu

COMBO 2

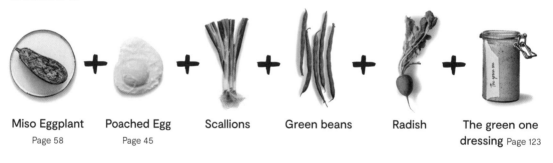

Miso Eggplant
Page 58

+

Poached Egg
Page 45

+

Scallions

+

Green beans

+

Radish

+

**The green one
dressing** Page 123

COMBO 3

Miso Eggplant
Page 58

+

Spicy Ground Bison
Page 70

+

Avocado

+

Cauliflower rice

Marinated Chickpea Combos

Packed with protein and fiber, these little powerhouses don't need much else to make a sensational dish. Add some healthy fat (such as avocado, feta, or salmon) for a winning nutrient combo.

COMBO 1

Marinated Chickpeas
Page 116

White Bean Hummus
Page 86

Feta

Tomatoes

PLUS corn, cilantro, herbs, dried chili flakes

COMBO 2

Marinated Chickpeas
Page 116

Salad greens

One-Tray Chicken
Pages 48–49

Avocado

COMBO 3

Marinated Chickpeas
Page 116

Foolproof Oven-Baked Salmon Pages 42–43

Roasted Pumpkin
Page 100

Parsley

Basic Chicken Meatloaf Combos

I use slices of meatloaf like toast. Grill and spread with avocado, feta, cottage cheese—whatever you love! Or crumble the meatloaf into a salad for extra protein.

COMBO 1

Basic Chicken Meatloaf Pages 52–53 **+** The green one dressing Page 123 **+** Avocado **+** Scallions

PLUS cherry tomatoes, herbs, lime, olive oil, chili flakes

COMBO 2

Basic Chicken Meatloaf Pages 52–53 **+** Perfect Roast Veggies Page 102 **+** Lemon + tahini dressing Page 122 **+** Basil

COMBO 3

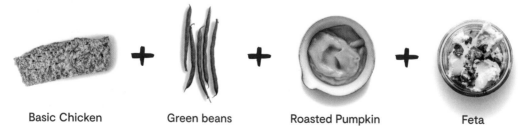

Basic Chicken Meatloaf Pages 52–53 **+** Green beans **+** Roasted Pumpkin Mash Page 100 **+** Feta

Index

Thank You

Firstly, a HUGE thank you to you, for picking up this book and for continuing to love what I do. I couldn't share my passion for simple, healthy food without your incredible support, so thank you for inviting me into your living room/kitchen/bed and reading this. Never stop investing in yourself and your health.

To the entire team at Murdoch (both in Australia and in the UK). You all deserve the biggest bloody high five and collective group squeeze. I'm grateful to everyone who had these pages cross your desk and annoyingly fill up your inbox. There were so many of you working tirelessly behind the scenes to pull this together, and I appreciate every single one of you. If nothing else, I hope this book makes a useful doorstop or computer monitor stand.

Dad. You've helped me become the hero of my own story. There is nothing I can do to repay you for your relentless, unwavering support and motivation at every turn. I love you.

Lee (@fitnessinthecity_), you are the best girlfriend and confidante a girl could ever wish for. Thank you for listening to me every damn day, celebrating all the highs, and picking me up when I'm down. Through heartbreaks, book deals, detailed discussions on my digestive system, and everything in between. You inspire me every day to hustle hard and aim higher. I love you to the moon and back.

Jesse (@jadammms), from changing your flights to hang with a stranger in New Zealand to all the incredible travel memories thus far, it's been one epic journey. Thank you for bringing a bit more balance to my life, and for inspiring the pumpkin pie recipe with those ten amazing days in the Canadian Rockies. You have made memories for a lifetime that I will never forget. I'm still coming down off that sugar high.

Sash (@livewithoutlabels), thank you for your consistent patience, nutrition tutoring in my time of need, incredible photography, and everything in between. I'm so blessed that you saved me that seat on my first day of class.

Jane M, from listening to my pitch (and telling me to come back with a better one—you lovely hard-ass!) to developing my idea and trusting me to shoot my own food. You had faith in this project from the word GO, and I'm grateful you took that chance to make magic with me. Thank you for your guidance and support.

Meg, for turning my images and words into a piece of art, being so on board with my vision from day one, and for the epic hand modeling and giggles on set. You have taken this book to the next level and created something I will still be proud of when I'm old and gray.

Jane P, thank you for your unwavering patience on this journey and the hundreds of emails you had to send to keep me on target and in line to get this project done. Your calm and collected way of getting things done got us over the line. Phew. You deserve a medal.

Sarah (@msmayohnaise), for your consistently solid work in my kitchen day after day. Not only did you follow my sometimes questionable recipes that needed a little more testing but you also kept me sane during a very intense four weeks. You even made it hella fun (with a little help from Sam Smith, too). I look forward to the day we work together again, gal. I wouldn't have done this without you, and would probably be another twenty pounds heavier.

To all my loved ones, for dealing with me during deadlines and late nights and for giving me words of encouragement when I needed them the most. Your unconditional support knows no bounds—thank you.

An Imprint of Simon & Schuster, Inc.
1230 Avenue of the Americas
New York, NY 10020

Originally published in 2019 in Australia by
Murdoch Books, an imprint of Allen & Unwin

First Tiller Press paperback edition January 2020

TILLER PRESS and colophon are trademarks of Simon & Schuster, Inc.

For information about special discounts for bulk purchases,
please contact Simon & Schuster Special Sales at 1-866-506-1949
or business@simonandschuster.com.

The Simon & Schuster Speakers Bureau can bring authors to your live event.
For more information or to book an event, contact the
Simon & Schuster Speakers Bureau at 1-866-248-3049 or
visit our website at www.simonspeakers.com.

Manufactured in China

10 9 8 7 6 5 4 3 2 1

Library of Congress Cataloging-in-Publication
Data has been applied for.

ISBN 978-1-9821-4346-6
ISBN 978-1-9821-4347-3 (ebook)

Publisher: Jane Morrow
Designer: Sarah Odgers
Cover design: Trisha Garner
Editor: Melody Lord
Photography and styling: Sally O'Neil (except pages 2, 7, and 208 by Sasha Leong)
Cover photography: Rob Palmer
Cover styling: Vivien Walsh
Food preparation: Sarah Mayoh
Production Director: Lou Playfair

Text and internal photography © Sally O'Neil 2019 (images on pages 2, 7, and 208 by Sasha Leong)
Design © Murdoch Books 2019
Cover photography © Rob Palmer 2019
Color reproduction by Splitting Image Colour Studio Pty Ltd, Clayton, Victoria
Printed by C & C Offset Printing Co. Ltd., China

MIX
Paper from
responsible sources
FSC® C008047

The paper in this book is FSC® certified.
FSC® promotes environmentally responsible,
socially beneficial and economically viable
management of the world's forests.